American Quilts

The Warner Collector's Guide to
American Quilts

Phyllis Haders

A Main Street Press Book

A Warner Communications Company

Warner Books, Inc.
75 Rockefeller Plaza
New York, N.Y. 10019

 A Warner Communications Company

Printed in the United States of America

First printing: March 1981

10 9 8 7 6 5 4 3 2 1

Library of Congress Cataloging in Publication Data

Haders, Phyllis.
  The Warner collector's guide to American quilts.

  (The Warner collector's guides)
  Bibliography: p. 15
  1. Coverlets—Collectors and collecting.
I. Title.
NK9105.H32   746.9'7   80-25304
ISBN 0-446-97636-9 (USA)
ISBN 0-446-97973-3 (Canada)

Contents

How to Use This Book   7

Introduction   11

Selected Bibliography   15

Color Key to American Quilts   17

Part I Pieced Quilts   49

1. One Patch   52

2. Four Patch   55

3. Nine Patch   58

4. Squares   61

5. Blocks   65

6. Bars   67

7. Jagged Stripes (Zigzag)   72

8. Diamonds   75

9. Chains   79

10. Triangles   86

11. Flocks of Birds   90

12. Sawtooth   95

13. Animal Tracks   101

14. Circles   104

15. Hexagons   111

16. Honeycomb   114

17. Stars   117

18. Suns   126

19. Log Cabins   131

20. Hourglasses   143

21. Bow Ties   147

22. Pinwheels   151

23. Drunkard's Path   154

24. Baskets   156

25. Fans   162

26. Trees   164

27. Alphabets and Letters   166

28. Yos-Yos and Puffs   168

Part II. Appliquéd Quilts   172

29. Chintz Appliqué   172

30. Flowers   178

31. Flowers in Containers   192

32. Wreaths   196

33. Leaves   201

34. Feathers   207

35. Buildings   210

36. Figures   214

37. Birds   217

38. Fruit   219

39. Hawaiian Quilts   222

40. Crazy Quilts   224

41. Presentation Quilts   231

42. Patriotic Quilts   239

Part III White Work   242

43. Stuffed Work   244

44. Overall Motif   247

45. Running Motif   249

46. Single Motif   251

47. Candlewick Spreads   253

How to Use This Book

The purpose of this book is to provide the collector with a visual identification guide to American quilts. To this end, an attempt has been made to classify quilts according to predominant decorative motifs and devices that are visually apparent to even the most inexperienced collector. The 47 different categories within this guide are meant to suggest a simple means of classifying the wide body of American quilts; they pretend in no way to be definitive. Quiltmaking, after all, is a highly individualistic craft that in subtle ways defies strict classification. But, given the number of books on this popular subject that are concerned only with how quilts are made or with presenting a gallery of pretty pictures with no interpretive analysis whatsoever, the need for a workable classification of American quilts, no matter how tentative, is more a practical necessity than ever before.

The broadest possible way to classify quilts is by **technique**—that is, by determining the basic method by which the quilt is made. Is the quilt made by piecing together small bits of fabric into pattern blocks, by appliquéing shaped fabric cutouts to a background, or by simply embroidering, quilting, or tufting a single or double layer of white fabric? These techniques—called, respectively, Pieced Work, Appliqué, and White Work—make up the three major divisions of this book. Each of these three classifications is subdivided in turn into component sections, some 47 in all, each of which is based upon an easily identifiable visual trait.

Because most pieced-work quilts are composed of pieces cut into recognizable geometric shapes—squares, rectangles, circles, diamonds, etc.—the quilts in this division (sections 1-28) are organized according to these basic geometric shapes and, in some cases, according to the basic patterns made from configurations of the geometric shapes that are virtually archetypal to the world of quiltmaking (Bow Tie, Star, Log Cabin, etc.). If the designs of pieced quilts are largely abstract, then the design configurations of appliquéd quilts, on the other hand, are mostly drawn from nature and are more or less realistically represented. Appliquéd quilts, therefore, are organized (sections 29-42) according to the most prevalent forms of the natural world that they seek to simulate (Flowers, Trees, Birds, etc.). White work, dependent for its effect upon its intricate stitching, is organized (sections 43-47) according to its predominant motifs and modes (Stuffed Work, Overall Motif, Running Motif, etc.).

The rationale for determining these three major divisions and their component classifications is fully discussed in the introduction to the major divisions: Pieced Quilts (pp. 49-51), Appliquéd Quilts (pp. 172-73), and White Work (pp. 242-43). In order to gain the full benefit of the guide, the reader should acquaint herself with the introductions to these major divisions, as well as with the introductions to the 47 classifications.

Once the basic information contained within these introductions is mastered, the guide is very easy to use. The book is composed of two pictorial sections. The first, the Color Key to American Quilts (pp. 17-48), contains 50 color pictures illustrating the three major divisions and their 47 component classifications. The second pictorial section, containing hundreds of black-and-white photographs, gives example after example of quilts drawn from each of the classifications. All represent quilts made between the years 1820 and 1930, and all are of the type available in today's antiques market.

Suppose you spot a quilt that appeals to you at a flea market or in an antiques shop. At first glance, it appears to be a pieced quilt, and it seems to be made up of a series of large squares, but it is otherwise unidentified. Perhaps the dealer has told you the obvious: "It is a Victorian quilt." But there are thousands of Victorian quilts. Exactly what kind of Victorian quilt is it? What is the name of its pattern? By turning to the Color Key (pp. 17-48), you will find among the fifty color illustrations a photograph of a quilt that bears a close "family resemblance" to the one you're interested in. Under the color illustration will be found the name of the classification (in this case, "Squares") and the page numbers in the guide that discuss and illustrate quilts in this category (pp. 61-64). By turning to these pages you will be able to find quilts of similar characteristics and information relevant to their type.

Using this visual guide, then, is very simple. To repeat: once you find a quilt that you want to identify, turn to the Color Key, find the color photograph that most closely identifies the classification of your quilt, and turn to the pages indicated for further information.

Each of the 500 quilts discussed in this guide is treated in a separate numbered entry containing basic information. A typical entry is reproduced on p. 10, together with a list of all the entities that are contained in each entry, from date and place of origin to material, size, and maker when known. Most of these elements are self-explanatory, but a few require a word of explanation:

Place and Date: Sometimes difficult to determine is a quilt's place of origin. Frequently the locale given in the entry may be where the quilt was found rather than where it was made. The true provenance can be known only when one receives a quilt directly from the maker or from her family, or, of course, if it is signed. Other attributions of place should be approached with a degree of healthy skepticism. Some quilts, it is true, do have specific characteristics that allow them to be assigned to a certain locality or even to an individual quilter. But most attributions of place are as difficult to prove as those of date. Too few quilts bear dates of origin, and even fabric styles—helpful in approximating age—are not hard and fast evidence of age. Scraps of material, after all, may have been saved for many years before they were employed in a quilt. Size may be an indication of date since bed sizes have changed over the centuries, but even this approach is not foolproof. More likely than not, a bed was a standard piece of furniture passed down through several generations of a single family, and a quilt may have been made for it at any time of its use. Basic design patterns may vary over a period of time, but patterns themselves are not particularly helpful in specifying the date of a quilt.

Size: Although the illustrations in this book are generally shown as the quilts would appear on a bed, some photographs have been turned to make the designs clearer to the reader. Size is generally set forth as length by width.

Price Range: This is a treacherous area, so let no one fool you into thinking that any so-called price guide is a completely accurate means of determining a quilt's value. Essentially, a quilt is worth whatever a collector is willing to pay for it. Still, there have to be guidelines, and this guide offers not prices, per se, but price ranges based on the following considerations: (1) that the quilt is in good condition and (2) that the colors are still true. The price ranges suggested in this guide are coded as follows:

A — $100 to $500
B — $500 to $1,000
C — $1,000 to $2,500
D — $2,500 to $5,000

Please note that the prices given are not necessarily for the specific quilt illustrated, but are suggestive of the type of quilt pictured. Two quilts, otherwise similar, may vary in worth because of condition, size, colors, date, fabric, and quality of workmanship, all legitimate factors in determining price.

Finally, the author acknowledges that any system of classification is at best an attempt to make simple the often chaotic complexity of the real world. There **are** quilts that employ elements that are both pieced and appliquéd; and there **are** quilts that incorporate more than one dominant design motif. These are not exceptions to any inviolable "rules," but proof of the richness and variety that beckon the truly adventurous collector of American quilts.

A Typical Entry

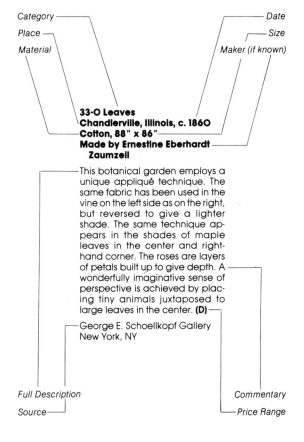

Category —

Place —

Material

Date

Size

Maker (if known)

**33-O Leaves
Chandlerville, Illinois, c. 1860
Cotton, 88" x 86"
Made by Ernestine Eberhardt
Zaumzell**

This botanical garden employs a unique appliqué technique. The same fabric has been used in the vine on the left side as on the right, but reversed to give a lighter shade. The same technique appears in the shades of maple leaves in the center and right-hand corner. The roses are layers of petals built up to give depth. A wonderfully imaginative sense of perspective is achieved by placing tiny animals juxtaposed to large leaves in the center. **(D)**

George E. Schoellkopf Gallery
New York, NY

Full Description

Source

Commentary

Price Range

Introduction

Collecting for me has been a very special treasure hunt. It began as a hobby, as a love of color, textiles, and design stemming from a career in fashion. Of all areas of collecting, I discovered, there is none more personal and captivating than that of quilts. Since beginning the search, I've seen thousands of quilts—some ordinary, some middling, some without expression, and many pretty ones. On the exceptional occasion a true work of art has been unfolded before my eyes. It may be an original design, brilliant in its composition and color sense, or a variation of a traditional pattern, the interpretation of a very gifted artist, perhaps a genius.

Hundreds of thousands of quilts were made between the last part of the 18th century through the beginning of the 20th century. It is easy to understand why there are so many when one realizes that often a young girl made twelve quilts for her dowry and a thirteenth when she became engaged. Quilts of all categories—appliquéd, pieced, white work—continue to surface everyday in shops, galleries, flea markets, house sales, and auctions across North America. Each quilt has a story to tell, if one could only trace its outlines. The creative outlet of quilting was very important to the women and men who exercised such diligence and imagination in needlework. In a different way the quilts have become just as important to me, not as a quilter but as a collector, and these imaginative objects of the past can become a significant part of your life, too, whether as a beginning collector or as an advanced one.

I would love to have known many of the gifted artists. What would they have thought if someone had told them that their very special quilts would someday hang in a museum or gallery—the Susan McCord quilts in the Henry Ford Museum; the Biblical quilt made by a Black slave, Harriet Powers, in the Smithsonian Institution; a breathtakingly beautiful "hourglass" silk quilt made by an unknown woman and hung in the exhibition "12 Great American Quilts" at the Metropolitan Museum of Art?

This remarkable "hourglass" (see 20-1), made in the early 1900s, was the first "great" quilt I parted with. It hung on a wall in our little house in Connecticut, but it was too elegant, too large for such a humble space. When I discovered a very similar small cradle-size quilt that I admired even more (see color plate 20-0), a rule was established in our household—I would always keep the one I loved the most and sell the other. The larger quilt was truly a "textile painting" and belonged in a museum, and that is how it made its way to the Metropolitan.

During the past twenty years, the great quilts of North America have achieved worldwide recognition as objects of considerable cultural and artistic value. Unfortunately for the collector, there can be no return to the golden age before discovery, to a time when a dazzling starburst or a colorful tulip design was used to cover a car or to line a dog's bed. Collecting quilts today means investing carefully in the best one can find, but collect only if you love these objects, and not because you feel you should. It is fashionable to assemble a quilt collection, yet it involves hard work and persistence. There **are** discoveries, nevertheless, to be made without hav-

ing to turn over a large sum of money. There is a special thrill in buy-
ing at an auction, especially one in the country, or in discovering a
dated piece of early fabric or even a quilt at a flea market. This does
not happen frequently any more, but there are people at the road-
side stands and small antique shows who do not have an interest in
quilts and want to sell them quickly for a small mark-up. Take your
chances and go out and look.

In my search I first began to return to the countryside I knew as a
child—that of Indiana and Ohio. I started running ads in newspapers
there before visiting friends and family. Upon arrival I was given the
notes or telephone messages in response to my inquiries and the
hunt would begin. With my mother, my aunt, or a friend I would visit
each house; I could not and still cannot refuse to look at a quilt. The
experiences have been wonderful and sometimes more than a bit
frustrating. At one farmhouse I saw a very large trapunto and appliqué quilt of an original strawberry design (see 38-1), and I was
thrilled to be given the opportunity to acquire this treasure. The
owner, however, could not understand my enthusiasm and further-
more refused a personal check. The bank was closed by this hour,
and I had to drive 150 miles back to my parents' home and return the
following day with cash. By this time, however, I had become so
deeply engrossed in quilt collecting that I would have driven many
more than the total of 600 miles that this one purchase had required.

Amish and Mennonite quilts had first caught my eye. Growing up
near an Amish community in Indiana, I knew something of the sect's
rules and religious beliefs. I also saw some of the quilts cherished by
the families on the infrequent days when they were being hung on
the line for airing and cleaning. Quilts such as these, illustrated
throughout this guide, have not been made, unfortunately, since
before World War II. I soon learned that fabric availability, the development of synthetics, and new kinds of dyes had brought an end
to an era of very special creativity. As I became more and more
aware of the value of the earlier quilts, I realized how much more I
needed to know about them. I began reading every new book on
quilting, to visit every exhibition, to talk to knowledgeable, experienced collectors and dealers.

I visited every available museum collection, studying and memor-
izing the fabrics, techniques, and patterns on display. Slowly but
surely I began to be able to date a fabric, to spot the places where a
quilt might have been repaired or altered. The stitches, so often sub-
merged in the play of pattern and color, revealed themselves as important details. Inferior quilting, I learned, is most often the obvious
give-away in a quilt that is only purported to be an early one. Prac-
tice in the art of quilting used to begin as early as three and four
years of age; it took years to perfect the tiny, even running stitches.

Every collector should always thoroughly examine a quilt before
acquiring it. Has there been any fabric replacement? If so, was it
done with a material of the same period and color as the original? It
is better that a quilt show its age than be altered with modern, in-
congruous materials. I have a magnificent appliquéd trapunto quilt,
c. 1840, in which the tiny yellow centers in red flowers are slowly
fading away. This is a quilt of generally fine quality, and its "ageing"
does not in my opinion destroy its value.

One important feature to look for if you are collecting cradle crib-

or crib-size quilts is the binding or the finished edges. If the overall appearance of the quilt is early, the binding should match. Hold the edge of such a quilt in one hand and with the other try to press the center of the binding toward the stitching. Most often the crease will appear slightly faded or worn and in keeping with the rest of the quilt. Early bindings on quilts of all sizes were often hand-woven tapes. If the binding was badly worn, someone may have cut off the edges and sold the smaller size as a cradle or trundle quilt. I once ordered a quilt—sight unseen—that was advertised as a small child's. I acquired it from a respectable dealer and he was probably as fooled as I was by the clever alterations that had been made. It was a very early central medallion pattern, and the binding was of the same fabric as the rest of the quilt. Enough fabric had been cut away and saved from the old binding on a large, full-size quilt, to apply to a new smaller binding. The give-away, once again, was the thread and the irregularity of the new stitching.

Do not be dismayed, however, if a quilt is very fragile. It may only need a new back to strengthen it. Silk pieces that are beginning to shred can be backed with a fine gauze to hold them in place. Amish woolen quilts often have tiny moth holes or other slight wear. One of my favorites, an "Ocean Waves" design, has what appears to be small rusty nail holes, and I suspect it was nailed to a barn door. What to do about such signs of use or age? Many of them, I suggest, can be ignored for the most part unless these visibly detract from a quilt's beauty or threaten in time to spread even further.

No one, nevertheless, can ignore simple dirt or stains which are very dark or large. Quilts can be very fragile and great care should be given to any attempt to clean them. Often the size will preclude hand-washing (machnes should never be used), for once the quilt is wet it becomes very heavy to lift. Cotton quilts of fairly recent vintage can be laundered in a bathtub with a mild liquid soap once a small secton of the quilt has been tested to insure that the dyes are color-fast. Stay away from bleaches, spot removers, or water softeners. A quilt is best dried out of doors under certain specific conditions. (Appended to the bibliography is a list of references on the care of quilts.) If a quilt is made of wool, dry cleaning may be called for; this is certainly the case with silk fabrics. In either case, an experienced professional should be consulted.

How should quilts be used today? That is entirely up to the individual collector. There is, of course, no more appropriate place for them than the bedstead. It is good to remember, however, that the best quilts were made for show, and that the housewife may have displayed them only in a particularly safe place and on special occasions. Quilts are now used popularly as wall hangings in homes and offices. Once again a word of caution on the fragile nature of many quilts is called for. Very special attention should be given to the proper method of display.

Care should be taken that the fabric itself is not damaged. The simplest manner for hanging is to fashion pockets of cotton fabric to the two top back corners of a quilt, sewing them to the strongest part of the binding. These pockets are then looped over the corners of a balsam wood stretcher or a single strip of wood. For a particularly heavy quilt, sew a 2½"-wide sleeve across the back at the top, slipping a strip of wood through this. If a stretcher is used, the quilt should not be pulled taut as this action may result in damage to fine stitching; rather, let the quilt hang as freely as possible.

Your collecting will be guided by the general availability of old quilts and by your planned use of them. Because quilts have become extremely popular in home decorating, there is a strong tendency to seek out those with the most striking and colorful designs—the log cabin, sun and starbursts, the startlingly modern geometric shapes of the Amish and Mennonites. But effect should not be your only measure of value. It is part of the magic of old quilts that out of a desire to create something practical and beautiful, so much could have been done with so little. Skills were developed to a high order in the hope of endowing something so simple with true artistry. The variations on the classic art of quilting are many—as this **Collector's Guide** amply illustrates; the possibilities to be enjoyed in this unique area of collecting are similarly plentiful.

A book that includes photographs of over 350 quilts would be difficult to compile under any circumstances. But when that book sets out to classify some 47 different categories of American quilts by illustrating prime examples in a systematic manner, the selection of photographs becomes an even more complex problem. I gratefully acknowledge, therefore, the cooperation of many friends and colleagues who permitted photographs of their quilts to be reproduced in this guide. Their names, and those of corporations and museums that generously allowed their quilts to be shown, are listed in the individual numbered entries accompanying the photographs. Special thanks are due Douglas Wiss of Tewksbury Antiques for helpful counsel and Helen Hamilton for organizational and editorial skills that are as effective as her love of quilts is affective.

Selected Bibliography

Alfers, Betty. *Quilting.* Indianapolis: Bobbs-Merrill Co., Inc., 1978.

Bacon, Lenice Ingram. *American Patchwork Quilts.* New York: William Morrow, 1973.

Bishop, Robert and Patricia Coblentz. *New Discoveries in American Quilts.* New York: E. P. Dutton & Co., Inc., 1975.

Colby, Averil. *Patchwork.* Boston: Charles T. Branford Co., 1958.

_____. *Patchwork Quilts.* New York: Charles Scribner's Sons, 1966.

_____. *Quilting.* New York: Charles Scribner's Sons, 1971.

Cooper, Patricia and Norma B. Buferd. *Quilters: Women and Domestic Arts.* New York: Doubleday & Co., Inc., 1978.

Finley, Ruth E. *Old Patchwork Quilts and the Women Who Made Them.* Watertown, MA: Charles T. Branford Co., 1971.

Hall, Carrie A. and Rose Kretsinger. *The Romance of the Patchwork Quilt in America.* Reprint of 1935 edition. New York: Bonanza Books, n.d.

Haders, Phyllis. *Sunshine and Shadow: The Amish and Their Quilts.* New York Universe Books, 1976.

Hinson, Dolores A. *Quilting Manual.* New York: Hearthside Press, 1970.

Holstein, Jonathan. *American Pieced Quilts.* New York: The Viking Press, 1973.

Ickis, Marguerite. *The Standard Book of Quilt-Making and Collecting.* New York: Dover Publishers, Inc., 1949.

Jones, Stella. *Hawaiian Quilts.* Honolulu: Honolulu Academy of Arts, 1930.

Khin, Yvonne. *The Collector's Dictionary of Quilt Names and Patterns.* Washington, DC: Acropolis Books, Ltd., 1980.

Lithgow, Marilyn. *Quiltmaking and Quiltmakers.* New York: T. Y. Crowell, 1974.

Mainardi, Patricia. *Quilts: The Great American Art.* San Pedro, CA: Miles & Weir, 1978.

Mann, Kathleen. *Appliqué Design and Method.* London: A. & C. Black, Ltd., 1937.

Marston, Doris E. *Patchwork Today.* Watertown, MA: Charles T. Branford Co., 1968.

McCall's Treasury of Needlecraft. New York: Simon & Schuster, 1955.

McCosh, Elizabeth. *Introduction to Patchwork.* New York: Taplinger Publishing Co., Inc., 1962.

McKim, Ruby. *One Hundred and One Patchwork Patterns.* New York: Dover Publishers, Inc., 1962.

Morgan, Mary and Dee Mosteller. *Trapunto Quilting.* New York: Charles Scribner's Sons, 1977.

Newman, Thelma R. *Quilting, Patchwork, Appliqué, and Trapunto: Traditional Methods and Original Designs.* New York: Crown Publishers, Inc., 1974.

Orlofsky, Patsy and Myron. *Quilts in America.* New York: McGraw-Hill Book Co., 1974.

Paddleford, Clementine. *Patchwork Quilts: A Collection of Forty-one Old Time Blocks.* New York: Farm and Fireside, n.d.

Peto, Florence. *American Quilts and Coverlets*. New York: Chanticleer Press, 1949.

_____. *Historic Quilts*. New York: American Historical Co., Inc., 1939.

Safford, Carleton L. and Robert Bishop. *America's Quilts and Coverlets*. New York: E. P. Dutton & Co., Inc., 1972.

Steven, Mapua. *The Hawaiian Quilt*. Honolulu: Service Printers, 1971.

Webster, Marie D. *Quilts: Their Story and How to Make Them*. Reprint of 1915 edition. New York: Tudor Publishing Co., 1948.

Books on Textile Conservation

Collins, Maureen. *How to Wet-Clean Undyed Cotton and Linen*. Information Leaflet 478, Textile Laboratory, Smithsonian Institution, Washington, DC

Guldbeck, Per E. *The Care of Historical Collections. Nashville: American Association for State and Local History, 1972.*

Hawkins, Mary, ed. Textile Handbook. 4th ed. Washington, DC: The American Home Economics Association, 1970.

Leene, J.E., ed. *Textile Conservation*. Washington, DC: Smithsonian Institution Press, 1972.

Removing Stains from Fabrics, Home Methods. U.S. Department of Agriculture, Home and Garden Bulletin No. 62.

Walton, Perry. *The Story of Textiles*. New York: Tudor Publishing Co., 1925.

Wingate, Isabel B. *Textile Fabrics and Their Selection*. 5th ed. Englewood Cliffs, NJ: Prentice-Hall, Inc., 1964.

Color Key to American Quilts

Part I. Pieced Quilts, pp. 49-171
(For general information, see pp. 49-51)

1. One Patch, pp. 52-55

2. Four Patch, pp. 55-58

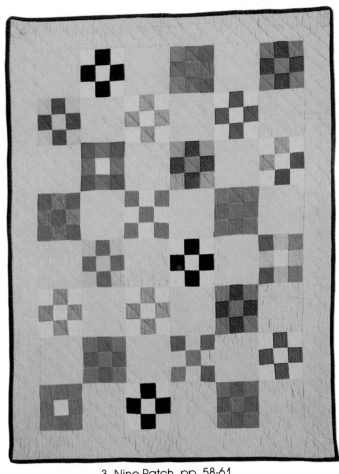

3. Nine Patch, pp. 58-61

4. Squares, pp. 61-64

5. Blocks, pp. 65-67

6. Bars, pp. 67-72

7. Jagged Stripes (Zigzag), pp. 72-74

8. Diamonds, pp. 75-78

9. Chains, pp. 78-84

10. Triangles, pp. 85-90

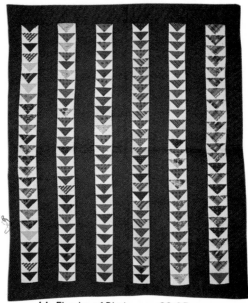

11. Flocks of Birds, pp. 90-95

12. Sawtooth, pp. 95-101

13. Animal Tracks, pp. 101-104

14. Circles, pp. 104-10

15. Hexagons, pp. 111-14

16. Honeycomb, pp. 114-17

17. Stars, pp. 117-26

18. Suns, pp. 126-31

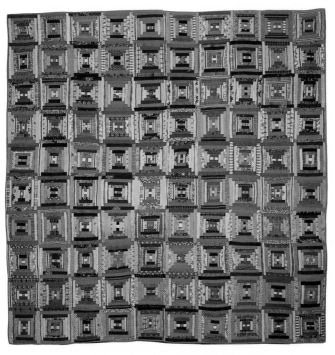

19. Log Cabins, pp. 131-43

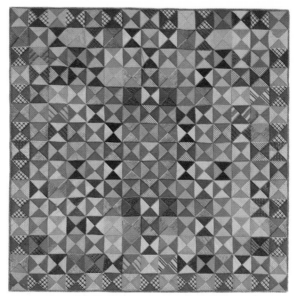

20. Hourglasses, pp. 143-47

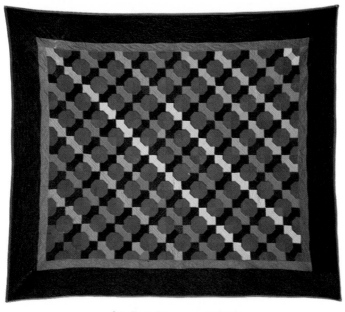

21. Bow Ties, pp. 147-50

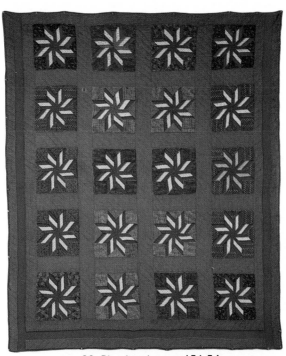

22. Pinwheels, pp. 151-54

23. Drunkard's Path, pp. 154-56

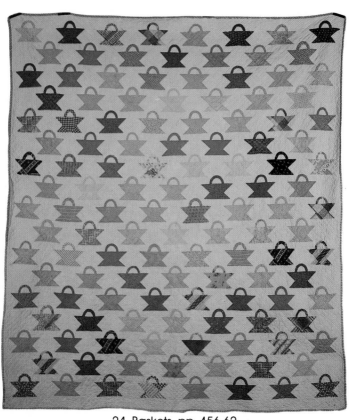

24. Baskets, pp. 156-62

25. Fans, pp. 162-64

26. Trees, pp. 164-66

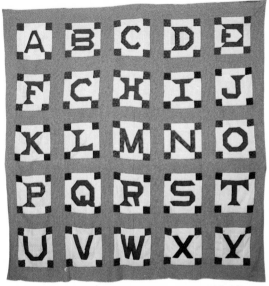

27. Alphabets and Letters, pp. 163-68

28. Yo-Yos and Puffs, pp. 168-71

Part II. Appliquéd Quilts, pp. 172-241
(For general introduction, see pp. 172-73)

29. Chintz Appliqué, pp. 174-78

30. Flowers, pp. 178-91

31. Flowers in Containers, pp. 192-95

32. Wreaths, pp. 196-200

33. Leaves, pp. 201-207

34. Feathers, pp. 207-10

35. Buildings, pp. 210-13

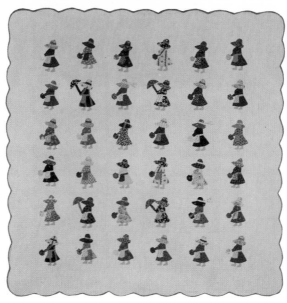

36. Figures, pp. 214-216

37. Birds, pp. 217-219

38. Fruit, pp. 219-22

39. Hawaiian Quilts, pp. 222-24

40. Crazy Quilts, pp. 224-31

41. Presentation Quilts, pp. 239-41

42. Patriotic Quilts, pp. 239-41

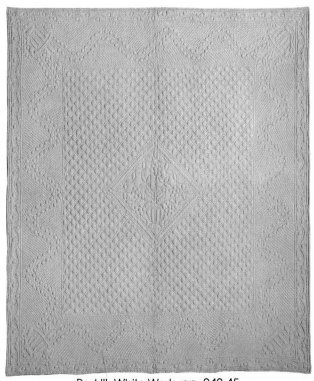

Part III. White Work, pp. 242-45
(For general introduction, see pp. 242-43)

43. Stuffed Work, pp. 244-47

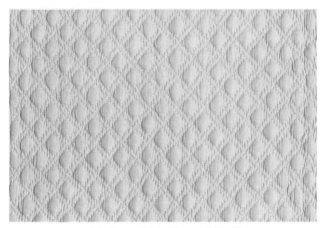

44. Overall Motif, pp. 247-49

45. Running Motif, pp. 249-50

46. Single Motif, pp. 251-53

47. Candlewick Spreads, pp. 253-55

Pieced Quilts

In recent years, the pieced-work quilt has gained in popularity as its wonderful geometric designs have captured the imaginations of modern folk-art collectors. Long before these quilts adorned the walls of museums, however, they were a practical necessity of American life and served to keep generations of our ancestors snug and warm during long winter nights.

Pieced work, as its name implies, is composed of small scraps of fabric cut into specific shapes and sewn together, usually into a pattern block. These blocks are joined to make the top layer of a quilt. Between this layer and the backing fabric is batting which gives the quilt its thickness and its warmth. In an era when necessity dictated that people save in order to survive, pieced quilts were created to use up the calico, gingham, plaid, solid cotton, and wool remnants from the family's homemade clothing. As more and more people prospered and wore clothes of silk, satin, and velvet, these expensive fabrics, too, found their place in the pieced-work quilt.

Pieced quilts appear to be made in an almost staggering number of designs, and the beginning collector might despair of ever making logical sense of the great variety to be found. Yet there are ways of systematizing the design motifs, or classifying quilts, once one recognizes that most pieced quilts are in part composed of pieces cut into recognizable geometric shapes—the Square, the Rectangle, the Diamond, the Circle, the Triangle, and the Hexagon. For this reason, the quilts illustrated in this section are organized according to these basic geometric shapes. In those cases, however, where the specified combinations of these shapes are joined into a pattern that is widely recognized as virtually archetypal in the quilting world (the Bow Tie, the Star, the Log Cabin, among others), the pattern (rather than the basic geometric shape that forms it) warrants a category of its own, especially since each of these "archetypal" patterns gives rise to its own set of variations.

With squares and rectangles among the simplest of geometric shapes, this guide begins with the simple Patches—One, Four, and Nine (sections 1-3)—particularly important for they are the basis of so many other designs. Section 4 deals with the basic Square itself. We then see how Patches are expanded and take on a third dimension in the Block patterns (section 5). Bars—essentially elongated rectangles—are illustrated in section 6 and are followed by designs incorporating jagged or zigzagging Stripes (section 7). The basic Diamond shape is then introduced in section 8, followed by a section (9) on Chain patterns. The progression from a shape (the Diamond) to a basic pattern (the Chain) is entirely logical since most of the Chain patterns are composed of small Diamond shapes.

Perhaps nine-tenths of pieced work could be included in the Triangle category (section 10), and making a decision as to just what would be covered here has been difficult. This section has been narrowed to include Triangle designs that are a composite of many triangles and do not create another immediately recognizable archetypal pattern such as Baskets or Trees. For example, pieced Baskets and Trees are made up of triangles, but are arranged to create a particular shape, thus warranting individual categories of their own (sections 24 and 26). The many patterns simulating Birds in Flight— each of them based on the simple Triangle—are treated in section 11.

Like Triangles, the Sawtooth pattern can be found in many pieced-work quilts, often as a border or as an edging to the design, but included in this category (section 12) are only those quilts whose sawtooth form is dominant and stands on its own as a design. Related to the Sawtooth designs is the popular Animal Tracks (Bear's Paw) pattern which follows in section 13.

The Circle patterns (section 14) are many and varied and generally exhibit the Circle motif clearly. Related to the Circle are the next two categories, where a fine distinction is made between the Hexagon (section 15) and the Honeycomb (section 16), distinctions that are discussed in their respective sections of the guide.

Having introduced the basic geometric shapes—Square, Rectangle, Triangle, Circle, and Hexagon—and some of the most recognizable pattern groups derived from them—Chains, Flocks of Birds, Animal Tracks, Honeycombs—the guide moves on to other categories that, although based on simple geometric forms, are well-known by recognizable pattern names. These include Stars (section 17), Log Cabins (section 19), Bow Ties (section 21), Baskets (section 24), Fans (section 25), and Trees (section 26), among many others.

The magnificent pieced quilt that begins the color section of this book (color plate I, p. 17) may justly serve as a "sampler" of pieced-work patterns. It is, in fact, a veritable lexicon of pieced-work designs, demonstrating the astonishing variety available to the skilled quilter. The quilt, made in Boston in 1854 of silk and velvet, measures 94 inches by 82 inches, and is reproduced with the permission of Phyllis George Brown of Louisville, Kentucky. A schematic drawing of the quilt appears on the following page together with identifications of the patterns and geometric forms that make up its component parts.

1. Four Patch
2. Pinwheels
3. Hourglasses
4. Blocks
5. Triangles
6. Chains
7. Hexagons
8. Jagged Stripes

9. Flocks of Birds
10. Suns
11. Nine Patch
12. Stars
13. Honeycomb
14. Squares
15. Diamonds
16. Circles

1 | One Patch

Every young child began to quilt pieced work by putting together a series of square scraps of fabric to create a very simple design, the One Patch. Variation was achieved through the diversity of fabrics employed and through the juxtaposition of colors across the face of the quilt. During the first half of the 19th century, many One Patch designs were chintz squares alternating with squares of a solid background color, a square of calico alternating with a square of chintz, or two squares of two different chintz or calico patterns. Sometimes the shapes were oblong, creating the patterns entitled "Hit or Miss" and "Brick Wall." In addition to the One Patch, the quilter could have employed the less popular, but equally simple, Two Patch and Three Patch designs.

1-O One Patch (Postage Stamp) (color plate)
Massachusetts, c. 1880
Silk and velvet, 62" x 56"

Scraps of fabric arranged in the Crazy Quilt design on the border are the same colors as those used for the small One-Patch squares making up the major design. The busy border adds a lively tone to the very geometric center. **(C)**

Judith and James Milne
New York, NY

1-1 One Patch
Ohio (Amish), c. 1900
Wool, 79" x 72"

Dark blocks of indigo and navy blue contrast with varying shades of burgundy, cranberry, and coral. Every other square has wreath tear-drop quilting or rose pattern. **(A)**

Esprit de Corps
San Francisco, CA

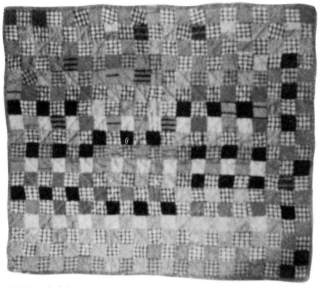

1-2 One Patch
Massachusetts, c. 1860
Silk, 16" x 13½"

In this doll's quilt, solid-colored fabrics alternating with plaids are naively assembled in this miniature design. **(A)**

Folkways
Indianapolis, IN

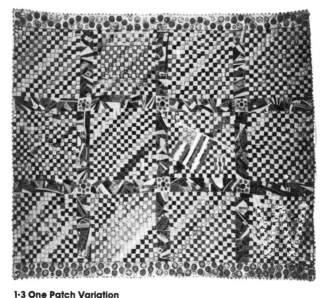

1-3 One Patch Variation
Ohio, c. 1875
Silk and velvet
Made by Anna Darst Peckham

This basic One-Patch pattern is divided in twelve squares by a Crazy-Quilt grid. Some squares are embroidered with a church, bouquets of flowers, a map of North and South America, and an eagle, flag, and crest of the United States. In the lower right corner are the initials WCTU for the Women's Christian Temperance Union. Small stuffed red circles on the bottom read "Anna Darst Peckham, Troy, Miami County, Ohio, Born 1835." **(C)**

Phyllis Haders
New York, NY

1-4 One Patch
Pennsylvania, c. 1870
Cotton, 84" sq.

Shades of brown, brownish purple, and red printed fabrics give
the overall color tone to this quilt.
Lighter shades of One Patch
pieces are placed to create a
diamond-shaped center with
spokes going to the four corners.
In the very center square is a face,
said to be of George Washington.
(C)

Phyllis Haders
New York, NY

2 | Four Patch

Of the three "Patch" designs illustrated in this book, the Four Patch
and the Nine Patch (section 3) were the most popular because,
once these designs were mastered, the quilter could progress from
them to more intricate patterns. A block of Four Patches could be
done in four different fabrics or could consist of two squares of one
fabric with the other two squares broken into triangles of multi-
colored fabrics. That more and more complicated patterns evolved
from these basic designs may be seen in quilts found in other sections of this guide. Flocks of Birds (section 11), Star motifs (section 17),
Pinwheels (section 22), Hourglasses (section 20), and Bow Ties (section 21) are just a few of the complex designs that can be broken
down into a simple Four Patch pattern.

2-0 Four Patch (color plate)
Pennsylvania (Amish), c. 1870
Cotton, 34" x 33"

After mastering the basic One-Patch design the quilter learned to
piece several patches together to create the Four Patch. Initials of
maker are in lower-left corner. **(C)**

Tewksbury Antiques
Oldwick, NJ

2-1 Four Patch
Pennsylvania (Amish), c. 1920
Cotton, 74" x 61"

The predominance of light-colored calico squares used in this quilt
gives the overall design a decided contrast to the very heavy burgundy red of the background and border. To the edge has been
added a thin white border which repeats the lightness of the center
design. **(C)**

Phyllis Haders
New York, NY

2-2 Four Patch Variation
Pennsylvania, c. 1880
Cotton, 82″ sq.

Minute multi-colored Four-Patch squares are interspersed with an occasional Nine Patch. An unusual border frames the design. **(C)**

Sandra Mitchell
Southfield, MI

2-3 Four Patch (detail)
Probably Illinois, c. 1890
Cotton, Quilt 65″ sq.

Each large block in this design can be broken into Eight Patches, which in turn are subdivided into the basic Four-Patch pattern. **(A)**

Private Collection

2-4 Four Patch
New Jersey, c. 1850
Cotton, 13¼" x 14"

This small block is a good example of how this design is created. Two squares of a brown and red plaid are joined to a square of a grey-brown print, and a fourth square of a yellow print completes the pattern. **(A)**

Newark Museum
Newark, NJ

2-5 Four Patch Variation
Pennsylvania, c. 1860
Cotton, 86" x 65"

In the squares of a purple grid are placed a variety of Four-Patch combinations in fabrics of chintz, stripes, ginghams, and plaids in earth-tones and reds. The design is tufted rather than quilted. **(A)**

3 | Nine Patch

The fundamental design of this pattern consists of three rows of three squares each, which appear the same whether viewed horizontally or vertically (see color plate 3). More imaginative Nine-Patch patterns have four small squares in each corner, a large square in the center, and four small bars on each edge of the block (3-3). Still more complex, yet clearly a Nine Patch, is the Double Monkey Wrench (4-5) or the Bear's Paw (color plate 13). Perhaps not as obvious, but nonetheless a Nine Patch, is the square of the Single Irish Chain (9-2); and even some floral motifs such as Tulips (30-18) derive from the Nine Patch. Finally, many Star designs evolve from the Nine Patch, as in 17-5. A helpful way to understand how the designs mentioned above relate to the Nine Patch is to draw up a grid of nine squares on tracing paper, drawn to the scale of the quilt. Once the tracing-paper grid is placed over an individual block of the pattern, the Nine Patch should be apparent.

3-O Nine Patch
Ohio (Amish) c. 1920
Cotton, 65" x 80"

The Nine Patch was the beginning "vocabulary" in quilt making, since it was from this simple pattern that young quilters experimented with more complicated designs, moving for example, onto the Bear's Paw (color plate 13) and certain floral appliqués. **(B)**

Esprit De Corp
San Francisco, CA

3-1 Nine Patch
**Lancaster County, Pennsyl-
vania (Amish), c. 1890
Wool, 87" x 80"**

Shades of pink and green compose the squares of this quilt, set against a deep purple field with a pumpkin-orange border edged in a very light purple. **(C)**

Phyllis Haders
New York, NY

3-2 Nine Patch
**Ohio (Amish), c. 1925-30
Cotton, 75" sq.**

A midnight-blue border with turquoise band and blue grid pattern outlines squares of red/blue, pink/blue, red/white, and green/blue. Some vertical rows are all done in the same color combinations, while others are punctuated with several squares of another color scheme. **(C)**

Darwin D. Bearley
Akron, OH

3-3 Nine Patch
Indiana (Amish), c. 1910
Cotton, 80" x 69"

Barely suggested in black and white is the subtle use of color in this quilt. The center is a putty color which is also seen as small squares in the Nine Patch design, as well as in the outer border. To brighten the quilt, another background color of soft lime/yellow appears just inside the edge of the larger border which is quilted in a rope motif. Bright reds and yellows and pastel pinks and blues with dark outlines offset the somber background color. **(C)**

Collection of Barbara S. Janos and Barbara Ross

3-4 Nine Patch Variation
Pennsylvania (Amish), c. 1920
Cotton, 78" x 71"

Variation of Nine Patch design in shades of pink, blue, and mauve, alternating with solid squares of blue, raspberry, purple, and shades of brown. Small triangle border is framed in medium blue with thin teal edge. Free-flowing feather quilting in border. **(C)**

Esprit De Corp
San Francisco, CA

3-5 Nine Patch
Newark, New Jersey, c. 1825
Cotton, 97½" x 102"

This popular pattern is created from printed fabrics in pink, red, blue, and brown against blocks of pink floral design. Framed in a sawtooth motif, the quilt has shell and diamond quilting. **(C)**

3-6 Nine Patch Variation
Indiana, c. 1880
Cotton, 84" x 78"

The design of this quilt is similar to that of 3-3, with the large center square tied rather than quilted because the entire quilt is stuffed—becoming more like a "puff" than a quilt. A ruffled border frames the design. **(A)**

4 | Squares

The basic shape with which all pieced work begins is the Square or Rectangle. Although these simple geometric shapes can be arranged in many ways, some arrangements proved so popular that they were given such well-known pattern names as the "Patches" noted earlier in sections 1-3. But there are other interesting patterns employing the square as well, the most simple of which is the grid of continuous squares, called, appropriately enough, "Squares" (4-3) and the large single square against a solid background (4-2). The latter, made by the Amish and Mennonites, are particularly handsome. Deep, somber, quiet colors in a simple square design become the background against which magnificent quilting techniques are displayed.

Other patterns—such as the "Complicated T" (4-4) and "Monkey Wrench" or "Hole in the Barn Door" (4-5)—are listed under the heading "Squares" because they are well-known patterns often placed within a square. In viewing the quilts in which these patterns appear, the eye will most often recognize the surrounding squares before it records the patterns contained therein. Another type of design that falls into this section in the Center Medallion motif (4-8) which is a series of frames enclosing a center design.

Illustrated in 4-7 is the very popular Amish pattern "Sunshine and Shadow" (also called "Trip Around the World" or "Grandmother's Fancy") which in this particular instance is arranged as a square. But note that this pattern can also be found in a diamond arrangement, as seen in 8-5.

4-O Square (color plate)
Ohio (Amish), c. 1890
Cotton, 38" x 30"

Crib quilt of blue and red has two large squares in center creating a simple, but handsome design. **(C)**

Phyllis Haders
New York, NY

4-1 Square
Ohio (Amish), dated 1907
Wool, 85" x 69"

A navy-blue quilt with inner borders of maroon filled with a myriad of quilted hearts and tulips was made to celebrate a marriage. **(D)**

Just Us
Tuscon, AZ

4-2 Square
Lancaster County, Pennsylvania (Amish), c. 1880
Wool, 70" x 80"

A stark, but handsome, design consisting of a cranberry-red center, black frame, and a burgundy border. **(D)**

Private Collection

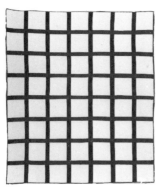

4-3 Squares
New York, c. 1900
Cotton, 88" x 79"

Orange squares appear solid but some squares have small white lines with minuscule dots of blue. The blue grid flecked with white frames the design. Simple hand quilting in straight lines. **(B)**

Kelter-Malcé
New York, NY

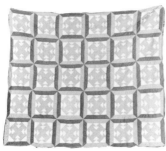

**4-4 Complicated T
Indiana, c. 1880
Cotton, 58" x 70"**

Gold crossed Ts are placed within a gold and red frame, lending a three dimensional aspect to the design. **(B)**

Judith and James Milne
New York, NY

**4-5 Monkey Wrench
Pennsylvania, c. 1880
Cotton, 75" sq.**

A blue grid flecked with small white stars surrounds these monkey wrench designs made from an array of fabrics in blues, reds, and plaids on contrasting printed backgrounds. **(B)**

Judith and James Milne
New York, NY

**4-6 Square with Star
Ohio, c. 1910
Cotton, 75" sq.**

Yellow background with yellow rolling stars (25) on red square with eight-pointed star. Border of yellow and blue diamonds on red band. **(C)**

Darwin D. Bearley
Akron, OH

4-7 Sunshine and Shadow
Pennsylvania (Amish), c. 1880
Wool, 71" x 70"

Shades of "shadowy" purple, mauve, blue, and green are punctuated with yellow, which gives "sunshine" to this design. **(D)**

Jill Haders
Mystic, CT

4-8 Medallion
Michigan, c. 1870
Cotton, 86" sq.

Surrounding a floral center motif in
putty color and red are a series of
sawtooth squares in shades of putty and yellow punctuated with the
surprise of red sawteeth randomly
spotted in the border. An edge of
yellow diamonds frames the quilt.
(C)

Sandra Mitchell
Southfield, MI

5 | Blocks

From the two-dimensional Square motif evolved the Block designs that are so cleverly pieced together that they give the illusion of a third dimension. A skillful use of color, combined with a sophisticated sense of design, resulted in these wonderful concepts of perspective. Sometimes these quilts resemble children's building blocks and are thus named "Building Blocks" (5-1), or the blocks may be arranged in a pattern referred to as "Stairway to Heaven" or "Stairs of Illusion" (5-4). Occasionally blocks are incorporated into a Crazy quilt (40-1).

An interesting aspect of these Block patterns is that one can turn the quilt upside down (as in 5-1) and still perceive the optical illusion achieved by a most ingenious choice and placement of fabrics.

5-O Blocks (color plate)
Pennsylvania (Amish), c. 1890
Silk, 62½" x 58½"

This exacting design required an experienced quilter to create an optical illusion combining squares. **(C)**

Esprit De Corp
San Francisco, CA

5-1 Tumbling Blocks
Holmes County, Ohio (Amish), c. 1920
Cotton, 39" x 34"

A crib quilt with top of blocks charcoal grey, sides purple as is large rope-quilting border. A deep indigo frame around the blocks and a tape in soft grey-blue edge the quilt. **(B)**

Kiracofe and Kile
San Francisco, CA

5-2 Blocks
Southington, Connecticut,
**   c. 1860**
Cotton, 47" x 39¾"

Stripes and calicoes have been
effectively employed to give the illusion of a pile of blocks. **(C)**

Smithsonian Institution
Washington, DC

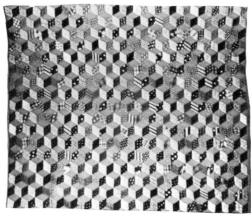

5-3 Baby Blocks
New York, c. 1890
Silk, 54" x 54"

Also known as "Stair of Illusion," silks in solid colors, plaids, stripes and
floral patterns give a vivid three-dimensional illusion to this taxing and
precise design. **(B)**

Phyllis Haders
New York, NY

5-4 Stairway to Heaven
Ohio (Amish), c. 1930
Cotton, 80" x 75"

A pyramid of blocks with a predominance of turquoise softened by beige, pinks, and mauve occupies the full dimensions of the quilt in this design. **(B)**

Darwin D. Bearley
Akron, OH

 Bars

Bars, of course, are elongated rectangles. In addition to the ever-popular Bar designs of the Amish (6-6 and 6-7), two similar patterns in this category are "Rainbow" (6-2) and "Joseph's Coat" (6-3). Both of these patterns tend to employ the primary colors and are alike in composition except that the "Joseph's Coat" pattern usually has a border around it while the "Rainbow" design occupies the entire surface of the quilt. The inspirations for these patterns—one Biblical, and the other from nature—are typical sources that American quilt makers turned to for their ideas.

All Bar designs are striking in their simplicity, a fact that can be readily observed in the quilts illustrated in this section—from the straightforward red and white "Bars" (6-1) to the slightly more elaborate pattern of 6-5, also in red and white, and the unusual Friendship quilt of 6-8.

6-O Bars (color plate)
Pennsylvania, c. 1880
Cotton, 84" x 80"

A straightforward design in three colors is enhanced by quilting with a diaper pattern in the dark green bars, twisted rope in the red, and a wave design in the orange. **(B)**

Mary Crain Bailey
El Paso, TX

6-1 Bars
Vermont, c. 1880
Cotton, 80" x 68"

A simple, but handsome, design is created in this quilt of alternating bars of red and white. Diagonal lines of quilting give depth to the rather flat design. Continuing the contrast of these two colors is the use of a narrow white tape on each side of the quilt and red tape at the top and bottom. **(A)**

Mr. and Mrs. Robert J. Bonner
Malone, NY

6-2 Rainbow
Pennsylvania (Amish), c. 1880
Cotton, 70" x 64"

A subtle gradation of colors from light purple to deep blue and from red through the oranges to yellow is evident in this quilt. These autumnal shades call to mind the straight furrows of a fallow field. **(B)**

Phyllis Haders
New York, NY

6-3 Joseph's Coat of Many Colors
Pennsylvania, c. 1900
Cotton, 84" sq.

Bars of red, lemon yellow, white, and light gray, blend into light blue, navy, and chocolate surrounded on three sides by white and on fourth by red rickrack design. Slanted outside colors are a repeat of these in large squares. Dark colors in center section quilted in a rope motif while light shades are cross-hatched quilting. **(B)**

Esprit De Corp
San Francisco, CA

6-4 Bars
Lancaster County, Pennsylvania (Amish), c. 1900
Wool, 76" x 62"

Intense saturated colors of gold, blue, green, purple, mauve, pink, and white are placed on a raspberry background with pyramids in clam-shell quilting interspersed with heart quilting ending in a light-blue tape. **(B)**

Esprit De Corp
San Francisco, CA

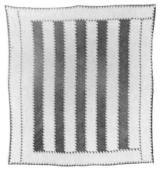

6-5 Sawtooth Bars
Pennsylvania, c. 1870
Cotton, 90" x 80"

Red bars with a sawtooth edge have been placed on a white background that leaves spaces creating additional white bars. Notice that the left side of the quilt has two rows of red sawteeth whereas the right side has received a different design interpretation. **(C)**

Darwin D. Bearley
Akron, OH

6-6 Bars
Pennsylvania (Amish), c. 1890
Wool, 81" x 68"

A green border with a thin red tape encloses red and mustard-colored bars that create a restful group of colors. **(C)**

Phyllis Haders
New York, NY

6-7 Bars
Lancaster County, Pennsylvania (Amish), c. 1895
Wool, 78" sq.

Blue bars are framed in a red square pinned by blue squares with a larger blue square in each corner of the border. A taupe border is filled with feather-quilting motif. **(C)**

Phyllis Haders
New York, NY

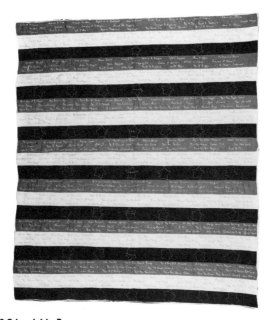

6-8 Friendship Bars
Little York, New Jersey, c. 1914
Cotton, 92" x 80"
Made by Ladies Aid Society of Little York Methodist Episcopal
   Church

Red, white, and blue bars with over 450 signatures and embroidered stars on blue bars. **(A)**

Tewksbury Antiques
Oldwick, NJ

6-9 Bars with Stars
Michigan, c. 1845
Cotton, 85" x 76"

Orange and indigo bars separate tiny stars in orange, green, and brown plaids. **(B)**

Merry Silber
Birmingham, MI

6-10 Joseph's Coat
Pennsylvania, c. 1875
Cotton, 84" x 80"

Vivid bars of blue, green, white, orange, and red are repeated across
the face of this quilt and framed with a striped border in the same
brilliant colors. For a similar quilt, see 6-3. **(B)**

6-11 Tree Everlasting
Pennsylvania, c. 1850
Cotton, 73" x 72"

Five white bars with sawtooth edges stand against a turkey-red background in this popular design also known as ''Path of Thorns,'' ''Herringbone,'' ''Arrowhead,'' or ''Prickley Path.'' **(B)**

7 | Jagged Stripes (Zigzag)

Included in this category are jagged designs resembling streaks of
lightning, some of which are quite lively while others are more subdued in their interpretations. Very subtle gradations of color are
achieved in the vibrant designs (7-2), making their movement almost
electric.

A distinction should be made between two closely allied patterns,
''Streaks of Lightning'' (7-4) and ''Straight Furrow'' (7-3). The ''Streaks
of Lightning'' pattern is made by piecing together two different colored fabrics on the diagonal to create a design with sharp jagged
edges. The ''Straight Furrow'' is one of the Log Cabin patterns (see
section 19) and is usually on the diagonal. The edges of this design
are limited by the ''log'' construction, making them smaller and less
pointed than in ''Streaks of Lightning.''

7-0 Streaks of Lightning (color plate)
Hamburg, Pennsylvania, c. 1910
Cotton, 76" x 72"

Pastel colors are placed like rickrack to resemble streaks of lightning.
(C)

Tewksbury Antiques
Oldwick, NJ

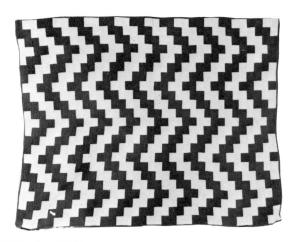

7-1 Streaks of Lightning
Virginia, c. 1880
Cotton, 76" x 62"

Stair-step blocks of red and white are built up into squiggling lines, creating the illusion of lightning. **(A)**

Judith and James Milne
New York, NY

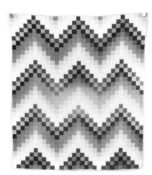

7-2 Streaks of Lightning
Ohio, c. 1890
Cotton, 80" x 75"

A great feeling of depth is created in this quilt through a very sensitive use of color. Starting at the bottom of the quilt, a triangle of brick red is outlined in black, then covered with khaki, abruptly moving into white, tapering off into pinks and light oranges, and ending in shades of brick red. This basic color scheme is repeated in bands across the quilt. **(C)**

Darwin D. Bearley
Akron, OH

7-3 Straight Furrow
Ohio, c. 1880
Wool challis, 80" x 67"

Upon first glance, this quilt appears like Streaks of Lightning (7-4). Closer observation, however, will reveal the squares of typical Log Cabin construction, done in a dark and light brown accented with red in the center of each square. **(C)**

Jonathan and Gail Holstein
New York, NY

7-4 Streaks of Lightning
Probably Indiana, c. 1885
Cotton, 81" x 72"

Flashes of lightning appear to streak across this quilt in a red and white zigzag stripe design. **(A)**

Goose Tracks Antiques
Knoxville, TN

7-5 Streaks of Lightning
Pennsylvania (Amish), c. 1910
Wool, 73" x 71"

Streaks of red and black lightning flash across the face of the quilt, framed in an avocado-green border in rope quilting. **(C)**

7-6 Streaks of Lightning
Place unknown, c. 1875
Cotton, 87" x 73"

It is hard to tell in this quilt whether it has red streaks against a blue background or blue streaks on a red field; either way it is a striking design. **(B)**

7-7 Zigzag
Pennsylvania (Mennonite), c. 1890
Cotton, 102" x 84"

The streaks-of-lightning motif is in brilliant red, gold, yellow, and black set against a midnight-blue field framed with a yellow sawtooth border on red. **(C)**

8 | Diamonds

Turning the Square halfway on its side creates a Diamond, a shape frequently employed in quilt making, but perhaps to greatest effect in the Amish "Sunshine and Shadow" design (8-4) made from an overall pattern of small diamonds. A very modern concept of color appears in these quilts, with red set against pink and purple, purple and green juxtaposed against dark blue, and shocking pink bordered by light pink, blue, and green.

Some of the designs featuring Diamonds bear the same pattern names as those employing Squares (see section 4), and for a very simple reason. Such patterns as "Crossed T" (8-7) and "Monkey Wrench" (8-8), for example, appear as frequently within diamonds as in squares. Once again, the eye perceives the Diamond before it recognizes the pattern within it. And for this reason, these quilts—no matter what the pattern within—are here classified as "Diamonds."

In addition to its use in the "Sunshine and Shadow" pattern and as a surround for other patterns, the Diamond is used to advantage in numerous ways—as in "Crossroads" (8-9), for example, in which a lattice grid creates numerous Diamond shapes, and as an allover Diamond pattern (8-10) that creates a fascinating optical effect that long predates Op Art.

8-O Diamond (color plate)
Lancaster County, Pennsylvania (Amish), c. 1920
Wool, 78" sq.

Light and dark colors have been pleasingly arranged in this popular Amish design, composed of small diamonds built up one upon another and forming a large center diamond. **(C)**

Phyllis Haders
New York, NY

8-1 Diamond
Lancaster County, Pennsylvania (Amish), c. 1900
Wool, 80" sq.

Red diamond with a pink border on a green background enclosing another pink border set in a blue background. A variety of beautifully-executed quilting designs can be distinguished; feather in the large border, petals surrounded by plainly stitched chevrons in the lighter borders, sprigs of flowers in the green area, and rosettes in the center diamond. **(D)**

Just Us
Tuscon, AZ

8-2 Sawtooth Diamond
Probably Ohio, c. 1890-1900
Cotton, 84" x 75"

Red and white sawtooth diamond within a sawtooth rectangle on a white field wiht a plain red border and narrow white tape. **(B)**

Darwin D. Bearley
Akron, OH

8-3 Sawtooth Diamond
Probably Ohio, c. 1890-1900
Cotton, 50" sq.

The sawtooth clearly shows up in two colors, here done in red and white. A rather straightforward geometric design is given movement by the zigzag edges. **(B)**

Darwin D. Bearley
Akron, OH

8-4 Trip Around the World
Pennsylvania (Amish), c. 1900
Wool, 75" x 79"

Ruby-red border with small diamonds of pastel blues, pinks, mauves, and greens flecked with white. Exquisite quilting, open center of raspberry with circle quilting and tiny baskets stitched in each corner. Feather quilting around the border anchored by a lyre quilted in each corner. **(D)**

Esprit De Corp
San Francisco, CA

8-5 Sunshine and Shadow
Pennsylvania (Amish), c. 1910
Cotton, 80" sq.

Small diamonds of calicoes and solid colors are arranged to give a three-dimensional aspect to this popular Amish pattern. The center square seems to be translucent. Dark border attached to a lighter frame is quilted in wave pattern of diagonal lines. **(D)**

George Kiberd
Ferndale, MI

8-6 Diamonds
Pennsylvania, c. 1870
Cotton, 84" sq.

A variation on the Nine Patch is seen in these triangles of blue, brown, and light purple. Calicoes are on a green background with green sawtooth border quilted to follow the sawtooth design. **(C)**

Sandra Mitchell
Southfield, MI

8-7 Crossed T
Shipshewana, Indiana (Amish),
c. 1880
Glazed cotton, 84" x 80"

Crossed Ts of mustard, light mauve, pink, and hazy blue are set against contrasting triangles in these colors, with the entire design resting on a rich brown background with a narrow brick-red frame. **(B)**

Sandra Mitchell
Southfield, MI

8-8 Monkey Wrench
Pennsylvania (Amish), c. 1880
Cotton, 34" sq.

A crib quilt of dark-blue wrenches on white squares on a yellow-beige background. Vertical quilting in center with diagonal quilting on sides. **(C)**

Sandra Mitchell
Southfield, MI

8-9 Crossroads
Maryland, c. 1890
Cotton, 80" sq.

A trellis (the roads) composed of blue stripes, dots, and squares, is laid on a red field creating numerous diamonds. Pink, green, and black stripes make up the border with rope quilting. **(B)**

Judith and James Milne
New York, NY

8-10 Diamonds
Pennsylvania, c. 1880
Cotton, 76" x 68"

Two different navy and white printed fabrics are used in this design. One print appears in several rows around the edge of the quilt and the other fabric is used for the rest of the diamonds in the center. This is a busy pattern that is constantly changing as you look at it.

Just Us
Tuscon, AZ

9 | Chains

The main patterns in this category are the Irish Chains—Single, Double, and Triple. These designs are rows of tiny Diamonds linked together, forming large Squares as the pattern evolves. Despite the simplicity of the terms "Single," "Double," and "Triple," the novice may at first have difficulty in recognizing the distinguishing features of those patterns. The simplest—the "Single Irish Chain" (9-1)—is easy to spot. It consists of one row of tiny Diamonds. The "Double Irish Chain" (9-4), however, presents a slight initial difficulty, since it is made up of three rows of Diamonds, two dark-colored outer rows and one central row in a lighter color. Only the **outer** rows give the pattern its name—"Double Irish Chain." Once this procedure is understood, it is easy to recognize the "Triple Irish Chain" (9-9), which consists merely of an additional inner row in a light color and an additional outer row in the dark color. The quilt made of Irish Chains was frequently one of the thirteen quilts in a girl's dowry collection. Other Chain patterns are "Job's Tears," "Burgoyne's Surrender" or "Burgoyne's Surround" (9-3), and "Chimney Sweep."

9-0 Chain (color plate)
Lancaster County, Pennsylvania (Amish), c. 1880
Cotton, 78" sq.

Red, green, and gold diamonds unite to form this triple Irish Chain pattern which is framed in a repeat of the colors in the center design. Each white space has a whorl quilting motif while the colored areas are done in thimble quilting. **(C)**

Tewksbury Antiques
Oldwick, NJ

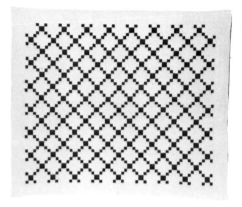

9-1 Single Irish Chain
New Jersey, c. 1910
Cotton, 69" x 59"

Blue and red diamonds are linked together against a white field. **(A)**

Tewksbury Antiques
Oldwick, NJ

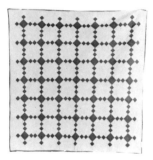

9-2 Nine Patch Chain
Kentucky, c. 1890
Cotton, 74" sq.

Enlarging the center square and allowing the white background to serve as alternating squares creates a chain design utilizing the basic Nine-Patch concept. This pattern is similar to the Single Irish Chain (9-1). A red tape picks up the red squares of the chains, quilted in the diagonal stitch. **(A)**

Judith and James Milne
New York, NY

9-3 Burgoyne's Surrender
Ohio, c. 1890
Cotton, 80" x 74"

Made of blue and white polka-dotted squares set against a white background with a scalloped edge on two sides, this quilt has a plain quilting in the main area of the design with twisted rope quilting along the edge. This design shows the influence of the single Irish Chain pattern (9-1). **(A)**

Kelter-Malcé Antiques
New York, NY

9-4 Double Irish Chain
Lebanon County, Pennsylvania,
c. 1900
Cotton, 82" sq.

Red and blue diamonds form chains across a white background with rope quilting in the border. **(B)**

Tewksbury Antiques
Oldwick, NJ

9-5 Double Irish Chain
Michigan, c. 1880
Cotton, 44" sq.

This cradle quilt of deep olive green with a pink chain and saw-tooth border has fine whorl quilting in the center of each square. **(C)**

Phyllis Haders
New York, NY

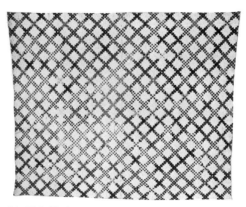

9-6 Double Irish Chain
Scipio, Cayuga County, New York, c. 1825-30
Cotton, 92½" x 74½"
Made by Jane Valentine

A variety of colors in half-inch squares are pieced to make this early 19th-century quilt. **(D)**

Smithsonian Institution
Washington, DC

9-7 Double Irish Chain
Pennsylvania (Amish), c. 1910
Wool, 86" x 74"

Burgundy background holding squares of pale blue hemmed in by deep khaki-green squares create this popular design. A tape of the khaki green binds the entire design. **(D)**

Phyllis Haders
New York, NY

9-8 Double Irish Chain
New Jersey, c. 1858
Cotton, 93" x 78"
Made by Sarah Ann Grover

A colorful quilt of red and green calicoes enclosed by a sawtooth border in similar colors. **(C)**

New Jersey State Museum
Trenton, NJ

9-9 Triple Irish Chain
Pennsylvania, c. 1880
Cotton, 86" sq.

This handsome design in red, green, and gold is framed in the same colors to create a very geometric quilt. **(B)**

Private Collection

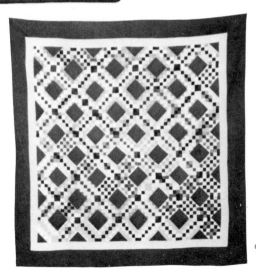

9-10

9-10 Triple Irish Chain

Ohio (Amish), c. 1930
Cotton, 75″ sq.

Typically, this pattern is composed of small diamonds in the same fabric linked in a chain design. This quilt follows this format, but does not
use the same fabrics in all the links of the chain in one row. By employing a variety of fabrics, the design is more colorful and a busier pattern
to follow than the usual Irish Chain. **(C)**

Darwin D. Bearley
Akron, OH

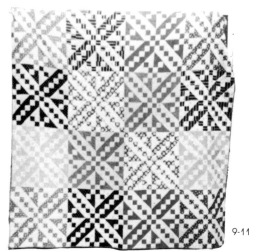

9-11

9-11 Jacob's Ladder Variation
North Carolina, c. 1880
Cotton, 80″ sq.

Although the Jacob's Ladder pattern is usually made of a light and
dark shade of the same color, this quilt varies the design by using red
indigo and beiges to form a chain design. **(A)**

Folkways
Indianapolis, IN

10 | Triangles

One of the most prevalent and versatile geometric shapes found in pieced quilts is the Triangle. The patterns using Triangles vary in complexity of design from a basic triangular form often placed on the diagonal (10-12) or horizontally (10-2) to the busier pattern of many triangles patiently stitched side by side covering the entire surface of the quilt (10-7). The latter design is subdued by the placement of cross bars to hold the design in place. This is perhaps the place to marvel at the innate design sense of early quilters, who, recognizing the "busy-ness" of multitudes of geometric forms, held their designs "in check" by framing them within cross bars, grids, and other devices for a "controlled" effect.

The fascination with the Triangle in creating an optical illusion manifests itself in several intriguing patterns (10-4 and 10-5, for example) that illustrate the dynamic designs that can be achieved by skillful manipulation of a simple geometric form.

10-0 Triangle (color plate)
Ohio, c. 1870
Cotton, 65" sq.

Shades of pink with sawtooth edge are enclosed in an appliquéd border of red Christmas bells and greens. **(C)**

Darwin D. Bearley
Akron, OH

10-1 Triangles
Indiana, c. 1910
Wool and Cotton, 88" x 80"

Solid purple triangles and inverted striped triangles alternate to form a pattern of repeating diamonds, half purple and half striped. **(C)**

Phyllis Haders
New York, NY

10-2 Triangle Trees
Connecticut, c. 1865
Cotton, 83" x 80"

A splendid optical effect is achieved in this quilt. Each triangle is made up of thirteen individual triangles of plaid, striped, or calico material. The composite triangles create the optical effect of white triangles in the background. The total optical illusion is of three-dimensional composite triangles standing perpendicular to the quilt. **(B)**

Judith and James Milne
New York, NY

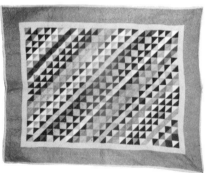

10-3 Diagonal Triangles
Ohio (Amish), c. 1930
Cotton, 70" x 65"

Mauve, purple, pink, black, and turquoise triangles bound by turquoise band and light blue border, edged in turquoise. **(C)**

Darwin D. Bearley
Akron, OH

10-4 Optical Illusion Triangles
Pennsylvania, c. 1880
Cotton, 82"

Calico, plaid, and solid-colored triangles are artistically arranged to give great depth to this two-dimensional design. **(C)**

Stella Rubin
Darnestown, MD

10-5 Triangles
Pennsylvania, c. 1890
Cotton, 75" x 72"

This quilt is filled with movement as colorful triangles are skillfully interposed against dark and white ones. A white and brick-red border holds the design in place. **(B)**

George Kiberd
Ferndale, MI

10-6 Railroad Crossing
Ohio (Amish), c. 1915
Cotton, 85" x 70"

Multi-colored diamonds in stained glass effect with black crossed bars, pinned by a light blue square, framed in light blue and black. **(C)**

Darwin D. Bearley
Akron, OH

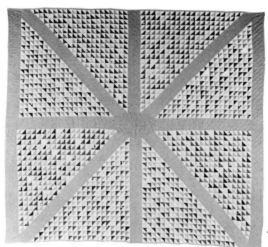

10-7

10-7 Triangles
Indiana or Michigan, c. 1900
Cotton, 13" x 12"

In this doll's quilt, soft shades of pink, grey, and green, with some deep earth tones, compose triangle shapes intersected by pink cross bars. **(C)**

Sandra Mitchell
Southfield, MI

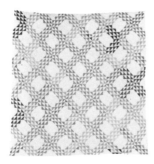

10-8 Ocean Waves
Missouri, c. 1920
Cotton, 77" x 71"

Blue printed shirt fabrics were used to make this design. Note that the quilter did not have a sophisticated color sense since she used occasional dark colors that weight the design in certain areas. **(A)**

Private Collection

10-9 Ocean Waves
Ohio, c. 1890
Cotton, 80" sq.

Small triangles of indigo against a white background create a formal interpretation of this popular design. The triangles around the border almost seem to be tucked under the center white section of the quilt. **(C)**

Darwin D. Bearley
Akron, OH

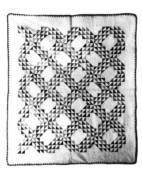

10-10 Ocean Waves
Wilkesville, Vinton County, Ohio, c. 1880
Cotton, 83" x 75½"
Made by Mrs. Mary Ann Bishop

This popular triangular design is enhanced by exquisite quilting that fills the border and center white spaces. **(D)**

Smithsonian Institution
Washington, DC

10-11

10-11 Arrowheads
Virginia, c. 1860
Cotton, 78" x 74"

Deep-green and rust arrowheads are lined up on a white field separated by rows of mustard-colored triangles. A double green frame border encloses the design. **(C)**

Stella Rubin
Darnestown, MD

10-12 Triangles
Maine, c. 1840
Cotton and glazed chintz
  105" x 95"

A large brown and pink glazed-chintz border surrounds sawtooth triangles set against a dark floral print background. **(C)**

Stella Rubin
Darnestown, MD

11 | Flocks of Birds

With nature the inspiration for many quilt motifs, it is not surprising in a land rich with waterfowl that "Flocks of Birds" would be a popular pattern for quilts. Twice a year quilters across America were exposed to the migration of these birds as they flew overhead—not at random, but following four established flyways in North America: the Atlantic, Mississippi, Central, and Pacific flyways. Flying in flocks of from 200 to 300 birds, 1000 feet above the ground in ever-changing patterns, these migratory birds captured the imaginations of quilters and were translated into breathtakingly geometric patterns.

Utilizing a Triangle to represent the bird, quilt makers placed these Triangles in a variety of arrangements whose pattern names changed with location and type of bird in a given area. Some of the more well-known are "Geese in Flight," "Goose in the Pond" (also called "Young Man's Fancy"), "Wild Goose Chase," "Hovering Hawks," "Hens and Chickens," "Flying Swallows," and "Birds in the Air."

Color plate 11 shows the "Flocks of Birds" pattern which is the simplest and most direct. A more playful design, however, is the "Wild Goose Chase," depicted in 11-1 and 11-2, where the quilter has captured a feeling of movement as these birds "fly" across the quilt. Note how this pattern varies from "Flying Geese" (11-7), a subdued and quiet pattern by comparison. While most of the quilts illustrated in this section suggest rather graceful formations of birds in flight, 11-8 presents a densely packed design—almost a virtually impenetrable cloud of birds.

11-0 Flocks of Birds (color plate)
Cumberland County, Pennsylvania, c. 1875
Cotton, 81" x 67"

Printed fabric triangles in hues of brown, rust, pink, and mauve are lined up in bars to create a feeling of motion which is balanced by the stillness evoked by the dark-green background. **(B)**

Tewksbury Antiques
Oldwick, NJ

11-1 Wild Goose Chase
Indiana, c. 1860
Cotton, 84" sq.
Made by Jenny Harmon

This graphic turkey-red and white design has twenty stitches to the inch in the quilting and was made by the author's great-grandmother. **(C)**

Phyllis Haders
New York, NY

11-2 Wild Goose Chase
Pennsylvania, c. 1880-90
Cotton, 80" x 75"

Movement in the red and white design seems to emanate from the small squares where the diagonals meet. A red border confines the motion of the main design. **(B)**

Darwin D. Bearley
Akron, OH

11-3 Wild Goose Chase
Cumberland County, Pennsylvania, c. 1880
Cotton, 88" x 80"

A raspberry grid encloses crosses containing triangles set in the Flying-Geese pattern against an olive-green background. A rather large printed border in a stylized floral design frames the grid. **(A)**

Tewksbury Antiques
Oldwick, NJ

11-4 Wild Goose Chase
Pennsylvania, c. 1880
Cotton, 85" x 75"

Shades of brown, beige, grey, and purple calico are subtly joined to create a somber quilt framed with a border of subdued colors in the main design. **(B)**

Darwin D. Bearley
Akron, OH

11-5 Wild Goose Chase
New Jersey, c. 1848
Cotton, 99" x 103"

The triangles representing the geese in this design are in red and white printed cotton placed in vertical strips. The design is framed by a sawtooth border with diamond quilting. **(B)**

11-6 Wild Geese
New Jersey, c. 1860
Cotton, 78" x 69"

This quilt top has a vertical band of triangles representing the geese, then a band of various colored cottons; this double motif is repeated across the quilt. Framing the design is a sawtooth border. **(B)**

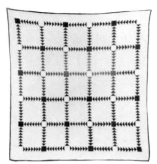

11-7 Flying Geese
Ohio, c. 1890
Cotton, 65" sq.

Alternating directions of rows of red triangles as they move around the white squares lend activity to this formal design. **(B)**

Darwin D. Bearley
Akron, OH

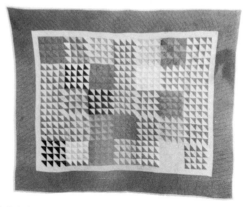

11-8 Birds in Flight
Ohio (Amish), c. 1920
Cotton, 70" x 65"

A bevy of birds seems to move across this quilt as one's eye goes from one block of triangles to the next. Shades of turquoise, teal, mauve, and purple are bound by a border of turquoise and brick red. **(C)**

Darwin D. Bearley
Akron, OH

**11-9 Goose-in-the Pond
Amsterdam, New York, dated
  1915
Cotton, 79" x 71"**

This quilt is a good example of how the patch design developed. The grid breaks the design into a Nine Patch. Each large patch can be conceived of as another Nine Patch. **(C)**

Kiracofe and Kile
San Francisco, CA

**11-10 Goose-in-the-Pond
Indiana, c. 1880
Cotton, 84" sq.**

Also known as "Young Man's Fancy," this design consists of a center square with a minute Nine Patch in each corner from which radiate two triangles; and where they join is a third triangle. Done in red and white, this design is interspersed with small Nine-Patch motifs in the white spaces of the background. The entire quilt is framed in a red and white square border. **(C)**

**11-11 Ducks and Ducklings
Place unknown, c. 1850
Cotton, 87" x 75"**

The geometric form of this design is similar to Goose-in-the-Pond (11-9) in that it is composed of a small square with triangles radiating from its four corners. Other names by which the pattern is recognized are "Shoe-Fly," "Handy Andy" "Corn and Beans," or "Hens and Chickens." **(B)**

12 | Sawtooth

Quilts in this category are composed of jagged designs resembling mountain peaks or the teeth of a saw. This category, therefore, should not be confused with the very popular Sawtooth design motif frequently found as a serrated edge on a geometric form—as in a Sawtooth Square or a Sawtooth Diamond in which the simple geometric shapes are given serrated edges (see 8-3, for example). The latter serrated designs do not appear in this section, but are to be found listed under the dominant geometric form (see, for example, Diamonds, section 8) because the Sawtooth in these instances reinforces the geometric shape and does not stand on its own as a design.

One of the most popular Sawtooth patterns, its name virtually suggesting the design, is "Delectable Mountains" (12-1), inspired by John Bunyan's **Pilgrim's Progress,** in which the range of mountains, covered with sheep, is a place from which to view the Celestial City (Heaven).

Although the Sawtooth is especially predominant in pieced work, it is nonetheless a puzzling motif as there is little precedent for it historically. Could it be an evolution of the pointed arch of a Gothic window or a development of the chevron seen in English and Norman Romanesque ornament? Clearly none of these is exactly the ever-present Sawtooth element found in American quilts, so we are left to wonder about its origin.

12-O Sawtooth (color plate)
Probably Ohio, c. 1860
Cotton, 76" sq.

Use of indigo and white provides a sharp contrast that clearly delineates the sawtooth design. **(C)**

Darwin D. Bearley
Akron, OH

12-1 Delectable Mountains (detail)
New Jersey, c. 1850
Cotton, quilt 96" x 92"

A red calico fabric was used to create these sawtooth "mountains."

Filling the white space is beautiful clam-shell quilting appearing like fluffy clouds around the mounts. **(C)**

Newark Museum
Newark, NJ

12-2 Sawtooth Crown
Indiana, dated 1866
Cotton, 88" sq.
Made by Mrs. Mary Lawson Ruth McCrea

This pattern is closely related to the Delectable Mountain design (12-1). The sawtooth of the main motif is reiterated in the double sawtooth border. A sampling of quilting stitches fills the white squares of the Sawtooth design. **(D)**

Smithsonian Institution
Washington, DC

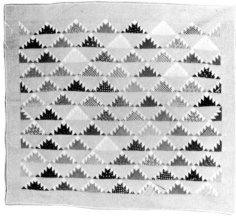

12-3 Delectable Mountains Variation
Ohio, c. 1880
Cotton, 75" x 70"

Pink background with triangles of grey, green, red, black, and beige prints with sawtooth edge alternate with pink triangles created from the background. **(C)**

Darwin D. Bearley
Akron, OH

12-4 Delectable Mountains
Pennsylvania, c. 1890-1900
Cotton, 75" x 55"

Breaking away from the patched or blocked concept is this design done in strips framed by small triangles gathered into diamonds. Only red and white have been used most effectively to create a variety of shapes. **(C)**

Darwin D. Bearley
Akron, OH

12-5 Sawtooth
New England, c. 1880
Cotton, 97" x 92"

Shades of brown, beige, and blue calico sawtooth triangles create an overall square motif. Edged with minute sawtooth border on white background. **(B)**

Private Collection

12-6 Sawtooth
Ohio, c. 1850
Cotton, 78" sq.

Done in indigo on white, this quilt is an evolution of the Nine Patch as the space of the quilt is divided into nine distinct areas. The jagged edges add a lively note to this very balanced design. **(C)**

Sandra Mitchell
Southfield, MI

12-7 Sawtooth
Indiana, c. 1900
Wool with cotton flannel back, 80" sq.

Shades of brown and beige interplay one against the other creating
movement in this quilt. **(A)**

Folkways
Indianapolis, IN

12-8 Sawtooth
Maryland, c. 1860
Cotton, 86" x 68"

This is a very complicated design. A set of white sawtooth bars on either side of a pair of diamonds creates a constantly changing design with contrasting indigo shapes. **(A)**

Judith and James Milne
New York, NY

13 | Animal Tracks

Although this pattern resembles the Sawtooth design in that both have jagged edges in their abstract compositions, it is listed here as a separate quilt category because of the popularity of its individual design motifs. Perhaps the most popular of these motifs is the one familiarly known as "Bear's Paw." It is interesting to note how this design evolves from the Nine Patch. (A cursory examination of 13-1, for example, will reveal how each unit of the design is divided into nine separate parts.)

As in the Flocks of Birds patterns, the names given the "Bear's Paw" are determined by geographical location. Long Island's "Duck's Foot in the Mud," for example, is known as "Bear's Paw" in Western

Pennsylvania and Ohio, changing altogether in Philadelphia to "Hands of Friendship" or to "Hands All Around" (a square-dance call) in the Midwest and South.

13-O Tracks (Bear's Paws) (color plate)
Virginia, c. 1840
Cotton, 96" sq.

An attempt has been made to color-coordinate the diagonals in this quilt. Starting with the main diagonal, from bottom left to top right, the basic color is yellow. The next diagonal on the right is blue, followed by blue-beige, concluding with three dark-brown diagonals, two beige, and the corner in yellow. The diagonals to the left of center do not keep as well to a given plan. Note the small tracks in each corner of the framed border. **(B)**

Kelter-Malcé Antiques
New York, NY

13-1 Bear's Paws
Ohio (Amish), c. 1920
Cotton, 97" x 73"

Indigo border with thin green square around paws of grey, green, soft pink, light blue, and four reds. A black grid separates the design. **(B)**

Esprit De Corp
San Francisco, CA

13-2 Bear's Paws
Ohio (Amish), c. 1890
Cotton, 75" x 43"

Resembling a Tulip design, these Bear's Paws are in dark to light blue set in dark squares against a raspberry background. Two sides of the design are edged in white sawtooth motif on indigo. **(B)**

Esprit De Corp
San Francisco, CA

13-3 Duck's-Foot-in-the-Mud
Knox County, Tennessee, c. 1880
Cotton, 86" x 76"

Each track-like pattern is in red with a mustard-colored center on a white background. The patterned area (top row) that would fold across the pillow does not have a row of red squares along the border. This design is also called "Hands-All-Around." **(A)**

Goose Tracks Antiques
Knoxville, TN

13-4 Duck's-Foot-in-the-Mud
Pennsylvania, c. 1840
Cotton, 92" x 80"

Yellow calico fabrics cut in the duck's-foot design are placed at the points of yellow diamonds, and the entire design is in a red calico diamond on a white field. **(B)**

13-5 Geometric Tracks
Probably Arizona, c. 1920
Cotton, 95" x 78"

Black and white footprints along a mauve path on white background with thin mauve and black border. **(A)**

Kiracofe and Kile
San Francisco, CA

14 | Circles

A writer in **Godey's Lady's Book** once declared that any quilt design using a circular motif is more difficult to accomplish than most other geometric patterns. With this in mind, one can appreciate the thought and labor that went into the execution of the many intricate patterns that could be made by employing Circles.

Included in this category are a great variety of motifs—from the solid Circle (14-1) to more ethereal designs (14-6). Particularly interesting are those designs that one might call variations on a Circle theme, as in the interlocking Circles of "Double Wedding Ring" (14-2) or in the sprightly motif called "Pickle Dish" (14-7), which was very likely inspired by reflections from cut glass. Other Circle patterns include the old favorite "New York Beauty" (14-11 and 14-12) and the rather complicated "Robbing Peter to Pay Paul" (14-5), in which the consistent alternation of the dominant colors may suggest the pattern's name.

14-O Circles (color plate)
Connecticut, c. 1920
Cotton, 81" x 74"

A playful and quite modernistic design is seen in these bright red circles against a white background. The edge of the design is in rope quilting, and the balls are reinforced with circular quilting. **(B)**

Kelter-Malcé Antiques
New York, NY

14-1 Circles
Pennsylvania, c. 1900
Cotton, 85" x 80"

White circles on a red background create a lively bouncing effect. **(A)**

Darwin D. Bearley
Akron, OH

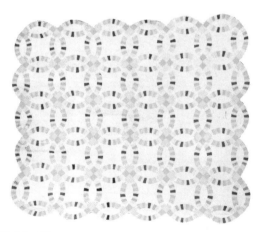

14-2 Wedding Ring
Missouri, c. 1930
Cotton, 72" sq.

Pastels punctuated with bright blue are typical colors for this design, popular in the early 20th century. **(A)**

Private Collection

14-3 Dresden Plates
Probably Michigan, c. 1900
Cotton, 84" x 68"

Circles of vivid primary colors with pink centers and border rest on an evergreen background. This pattern is also known as "Friendship Circle," "Friendship Ring," and "Aster." **(A)**

Mayeve Tate
Princeton, NJ

14-4 Dresden Plate
Ohio, c. 1920
Cotton, 42" x 24"

Crib quilt of plates in fabric typical of 1920s with pink centers and scalloped edge with pink border. **(A)**

Judith and James Milne
New York, NY

14-5 Robbing Peter to Pay Paul
Pennsylvania (Amish), c. 1910
Cotton, 77" x 65"

Bright blue and red solid fabrics are pieced together to create this popular but complicated pattern. Diagonal crosses are quilted in the center of each design and large fan quilting fills the border. **(B)**

Collection of Barbara S. Janos and Barbara Ross
New York, NY

14-6 Circle
Ohio, c. 1870
Cotton, 74" x 68"

A blue and green cotton print border contrasts with this rather stark circle design in pale moss green. Interrupting the design in each corner are silhouetted sprigs of flowers and leaves in the same green as the circle. **(B)**

Kelter-Malcé Antiques
New York, NY

14-7 Pickle Dish
Ohio, c. 1890-1900
Cotton, 65" sq.

A bright yellow background with an indigo square border, red pinwheels between pickle dishes in indigo on white. **(B)**

Darwin D. Bearley
Akron, OH

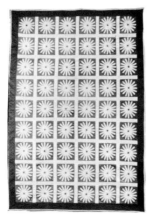

14-8 Compass
Ohio, c. 1890
Cotton, 103¾" x 73"

Presented to Charles H. Stocking (b. 1843-d. 1926), minister of an Ohio Methodist church, by the members. Made to raise money; names written on quilt for 25¢ donation. Fifty-four squares, white with spiked circles appliquéd on red squares. **(C)**

Smithsonian Institution
Washington, DC

14-9 Mariner's Compass
Ohio, c. 1870-80
Cotton, 65" sq.

Blue and white compass in blue grid on white background with serpentine appliqué border. **(C)**

Darwin D. Bearley
Akron, OH

14-9

14-10 Mariner's Compass (Variation)
Probably Ohio, c. 1870
Cotton, 90" x 80"

Twenty circles of dark to light green with pink center and green tail on a white background with green band and sawtooth border. **(C)**

Darwin D. Bearley
Akron, OH

14-11 New York Beauty
Probably New England, c. 1880
Cotton, 76" x 65"

Also known as "Crown of Thorns" or "Rocky Mountain Road," this design is frequently done in only two colors, in this case, red and white. **(C)**

Mildred Barnes
Mystic, CT

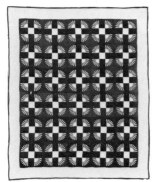

14-12 New York Beauty
Pennsylvania, c. 1880
Cotton, 85" x 70"

White circles broken by an indigo
grid are pinned in place with a
white square. A white border is
edged with an indigo tape. **(C)**

Kelter-Malcé Antiques
New York, NY

14-13 Melon with Star
Maine, c. 1910
Cotton, 80" x 78"

The stars are grey and white fabric with blue cornflowers or a red corn-
flower design on charcoal grey. The melons are made of strips of
brown and red fabric with white and some green accents. **(A)**

Kelter-Malcé Antiques
New York, NY

15 | Hexagons

A Hexagon, of course, is a six-sided figure, and is very frequently used as an important element in quilt design. This section includes quilts which employ **widely-spaced** Hexagons which sometimes appear in rows resembling mosaic tile (15-5) or are grouped to form large Hexagons-within-Hexagons (15-4) or even a single large Hexagon (color plate 15).

Interlocking Hexagons make up a series of patterns known as "Honeycombs" and are treated separately in section 16.

15-O Hexagon (color plate)
Pennsylvania, c. 1850
Cotton, 78" sq.

A medley of six-sided pieces has been put together creatively into mosaic and bar designs. **(B)**

Sandra Mitchell
Southfield, MI

15-1 Grandmother's Flower Garden
Indiana, c. 1880
Wool, 80" sq.

Hexagons of a beige chintz are arranged in a rope effect around hexagons of brick red with white rosettes in a beige and red grid. Diamond quilting in the brick-red background is set off by a bright yellow tape. **(C)**

Darwin D. Bearley
Akron, OH

15-2 Flower Garden
Probably Connecticut, c. 1840
Cotton, 32" x 33"

Red and green hexagons with pink centers rest on a white background that is quilted in hexagons. A delicate vine of stuffed flowers meanders along the border. **(C)**

Phyllis Haders
New York, NY

15-3 Flower Garden
Michigan, c. 1930
Cotton, 90" x 78"
Made by Minna Stienke

Pastel "flowers" with yellow centers on a white background are edged in a deep and light pink border, two sides of which are a sawtooth design. **(A)**

Mayeve Tate
Princeton, NJ

15-4 Hexagon with Chintz Border
New York, c. 1820
Cotton, 106" x 94"

Small hexagons with eight-pointed stars in them are joined together in a series of larger hexagonal designs. The white areas are filled with a variety of stuffed motifs. **(C)**

Jo Giese Brown
New York, NY

15-4

15-5

15-5 Hexagon
Ohio, c. 1900
Satin and velvet, 60" x 50"

A black background supports earth-tone hexagons pinned by a black center. Brightly-colored stripes frame the design. **(A)**

Folkways
Indianapolis, IN

15-6 Spider or Cobweb
West Virginia, c. 1890
Wool, 80" sq.

Although employing octagons, this quilt in somber wools is larger in scale than the usual hexagon-design quilt, but follows that basic design technique. **(A)**

Judith and James Milne
New York, NY

16 | Honeycomb

Similar to the Hexagon is the Honeycomb design. It, too, is composed of small Hexagons united in a collection of larger six-sided shapes which are then pieced together side by side to resemble the cross section of a honeycomb. The Honeycomb design is therefore a complex of numerous Hexagons that fill the quilt. In some quilts of this design the individual parts are minute, measuring less than half an inch in diameter.

16-0 Honeycomb (color plate)
Shipshewana, Indiana, c. 1890
Wool, 84" x 81"

A honeycomb design is made from small hexagons of mauve, blue, pink, and brown, outlined by small turquoise diamonds with a scalloped border on one end. **(C)**

Phyllis Haders

16-1

16-1 Honeycomb
Place unknown, c. 1830
Cotton, 93½" x 70½"

Mustard-colored hexagons with white centers encircled with green chintz in an organized design filling the entire quilt. **(A)**

Smithsonian Institution

16-2

16-2 Honeycomb Rose
Place unknown, c. 1860
Cotton, 95" x 71"

A delicately embroidered rose in the center is surrounded by hexagonal stars. The border picks up the floral motif with embroidered roses in each corner and a vine design along the sides. **(C)**

Smithsonian Institution

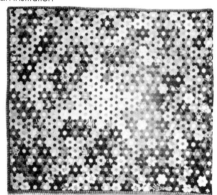

16-3

16-3 Honeycomb
Place unknown, c. 1880
Silk and wool, 71½" x 62½"
Made by Martha Mahetable and Lucena Beardley Kile.

Small multi-colored hexagons sewn together in rosettes are scattered across the full surface of the quilt. **(C)**

Smithsonian Institution

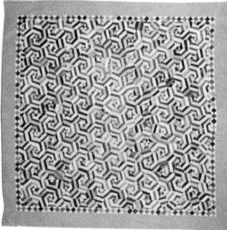

16-4

16-4 Honeycomb
Pennsylvania, c. 1880
Cotton, 80" x 75"

A pink print border encloses angular shapes in various shades of pink, brown, beige, and mauve punctuated with bars of white and black. Small diamonds separate the border from the overall pattern center. **(C)**

Darwin D. Bearley
Akron, OH

16-5 Garden Maze
Ohio, c. 1880
Cotton, 80" x 75"

Hexagons of crossed indigo bars with four modified flower baskets in each corner of hexagon. Fine diamond pattern quilting in white section of each hexagon. **(C)**

Darwin D. Bearley
Akron, OH

17 | Stars

There is perhaps no single design in the entire vocabulary of pieced work that has produced more different names than the Star. Some authorities claim that over 100 different Star patterns have been identified. With names derived from nature, the Bible, and politics, this motif is known by such favorite appellations as "Lone Star," "Evening Star," "Star of Bethlehem," "Blazing Star," "Twinkling Star," "Star of the East," "Star of Le Moyne" or "Lemon Star," "Union Star," and "Star-Spangled Banner." There are as well Stars named for various states and towns: "Texas Star," "California Star," "Chicago Star," and "St. Louis Star," to name just a few. As varied as the names, are the designs themselves. Some feature one large Star occupying the whole field of the quilt (17-1). Others consist of four Stars that touch (17-12); many Stars sprinkled over the surface of the quilt (17-11); large Stars mixed with smaller Stars; and many other designs often interspersed with other motifs (17-6).

This quilt category features Stars with very pronounced and well-defined points. It should not be confused with the Sunbursts (sometimes called Starbursts) found in the next section.

17-O Starburst (color plate)
Pennsylvania, c. 1880
Wool, 92½" x 91"

Appliquéd birds in colors derived from the starburst add lively movement around a vibrant pieced star. This busy design is held in place by the staid geometrically-conceived baskets.

Just Us
Tucson, AZ

17-1 Star of Bethlehem
Vermont, c. 1880
Cotton, 84" sq.

This typical star pattern is enhanced by blocks around the edge, giving depth to the design. Interlocking quilting patterns make a border along the top and bottom with some of the same designs placed between the points of the star. **(C)**

Mr. and Mrs. Robert J. Bonner
Malone, NY

17-2 Star of Bethlehem
Missouri, c. 1920
Cotton, 77" x 71"

Blue and white shirt material in the shape of diamonds and chevrons are fitted together to make this popular design. Four star clusters in the corners add a quieting note to this pulsating design. **(B)**

Private Collection

17-3 Star of Bethlehem
Lehigh County, Pennsylvania (Mennonite), c. 1880
Cotton, 84" sq.

The dark colors of this quilt are brown and pink, alternating with a very pale yellow and white. The interlocking chevrons are actually eight-pointed stars whose lighter points fade into the background. **(B)**

Tewksbury Antiques
Oldwick, NJ

17-3

17-4 Star
Pennsylvania (Mennonite),
  c. 1870
Cotton, 76" sq.

Blue, red, white, orange, and indigo diamonds create this star
pattern placed on an indigo
background which contains red
and white stars. **(B)**

Phyllis Haders
New York, NY

17-5 Lone Star
Pennsylvania (Amish), c. 1900
Cotton, 67" sq.

Crib quilt with center star in gold
followed by grey, burgundy, and
blue (then repeated) set against a
ground of blue with a yellow and
burgundy frame against a grey
background with yellow edge.
Diamond quilting pattern in the
background. **(C)**

Kelter-Malcé Antiques
New York, NY

17-6 Lone Star Variation
Ohio, c. 1850-60
Cotton, 90" sq.

Tip of star starts with red, yellow, white, and green with rings of red/white/red. Center is green, yellow, and red. Appliquéd rosettes and leaves are placed between the points of star while a meandering vine and flower border completes the design. **(C)**

Darwin D. Bearley
Akron, OH

17-7 Lone Star
Ohio, c. 1870
Cotton, 75" sq.

Eight-pointed star of red, yellow, green, brown, and pink with smaller stars in each corner and half stars on each side and at the top and bottom. Green, rust, and black bars frame the design. **(C)**

Darwin D. Bearley
Akron, OH

17-8 Lone Star Variation
Massachusetts, c. 1900
Cotton, 80" x 75"

Star is beige, brown, and red with accents of black. Turquoise squares in four corners with two shades of turquoise bands around border. **(C)**

Darwin D. Bearley
Akron, OH

17-9 Broken Star
Lancaster County, Pennsylvania, c. 1910
Cotton, 82" sq.

Outer points of star are pale pink, dark green, then shading from deep pink to white and ending in deep pink and pumpkin. These colors are repeated in center star with background of white and deep-pink edge. **(C)**

Tewksbury Antiques
Oldwick, NJ

17-10 Blazing Stars
Ohio (Amish), c. 1850
Cotton, 87" x 71"

A midnight-blue frame around the design next to bright olive green held in place by bars of midnight blue on each side with a binding of the olive green draws one's attention to the border as much as to the design done in brick-red stars encircled with forest-green geometric wreaths. **(C)**

Sandra Mitchell
Southfield, MI

17-11 Twinkling Star
Funkstown, Maryland, c. 1840
Cotton, 94" x 92"
Made by Ann Sophie Shriver

Sixteen circles of multi-colored cotton prints on bleached muslin background. Princess feather quilting is between the suns with a running feather in the border framed by calico sawtooth. **(D)**

Smithsonian Institution
Washington, DC

17-12 Touching Stars of Bethlehem
Ohio, c. 1870
Cotton, 65" sq.

Yellow background holds stars of brown, yellow, blue, and mauve with appliquéd border in brown. Small brown stars are interspersed among large stars. **(C)**

Darwin D. Bearley
Akron, OH

17-13 Feathered Star
New York, c. 1885
Cotton, 78" x 69"

Red feathered stars on a white background with red and white grid anchored in center with Nine Patch in four corners. **(B)**

Mr. and Mrs. Robert J. Bonner
Malone, NY

17-14 Feathered Star
New York, c. 1880
Cotton, 78" sq.

Blue calico squares are built up with jagged edges topped by a diamond point evolving into a star. The stars, in turn, make interesting shapes out of the white spaces. **(B)**

Tewksbury Antiques
Oldwick, NJ

17-15 Feathered Star Variation
Ohio, c. 1870
Cotton, 85" sq.

Indigo-blue stars on white background with zigzag border. **(C)**

Darwin D. Bearley
Akron, OH

17-16 Feathered Stars
Ohio, c. 1870
Cotton, 95" x 80"

Square with star points of green and red tints surrounded on three sides

17-16

by green swag appliquéd border. Main design interspersed with small red and green plaid stars. **(C)**

Darwin D. Bearley
Akron, OH

17-17 Stars in Grid
Ohio, c. 1880
Cotton, 86" sq.

17-17

Double Le Moyne stars within a sawtooth star are squared off by a garden-maze grid. Tips of large stars are of grid fabric as is sawtooth within the star. Pink fills in the points and shades of brown, beige, and white are the colors in the Le Moyne star. **(C)**

Phyllis Haders
New York, NY

17-18

17-18 Stars in Grid
Gettysburg, Pennsylvania, c. 1860
Cotton, 102" sq.

Border of pink peonies with blue leaves and a grid of red printed fabric enclose stars of red, brown, and green. White background with quilting motifs of flowers and leaves. **(C)**

Jo Giese Brown
New York, NY

18 | Suns

Often Star and Sun designs will bear the same common pattern name, a fact which frequently makes it difficult to determine the dif-

ference between a Star and Sun. In this guide, a Star is a design that has quite clearly-defined points (see section 17), while a Sun creates a bursting effect that occupies the full dimensions of the quilt (see, for example, 18-1). The easiest way to comprehend the Sun (or Sunburst) design is that it is essentially an enlarged body of a Star **without the points.**

Sun patterns are vigorous in their total effect and display an ingenious skill in organizing fabrics so that they impart an impression of fiery sun rays.

18-O Sunburst (color plate)
Pennsylvania, c. 1880
Cotton, 54" sq.

The deeply saturated colors are united with the background by the three rings of white in the sunburst design. Beautiful rope-pattern quilting frames delicately-quilted leaves around the sun. **(C)**

Phyllis Haders
New York, NY

18-1 Sunburst
Pennsylvania, c. 1900
Cotton, 84" x 82"

A brilliant red border surrounds a blue, green, red, and white sunburst with red and yellow flowers and flowerpots appliquéd in corners of the blue-green background. **(C)**

Just Us
Tucson, AZ

18-2 Sunburst
Pennsylvania, c. 1900
Cotton, 42" sq.

This cradle quilt with rings of pink, yellow, orange, and red is subdued by darker rings in shades of khaki, and the whole design is confined by a vivid red border. **(C)**

Phyllis Haders
New York, NY

18-3 Blazing Sun
Ohio, c. 1880
Cotton, 80" x 75"

Dark bands of green and brown alternating with yellow and white form the sun. A dark green and brown diamond border encloses the sun and fans of sawtooth in each corner. **(C)**

Darwin D. Bearley
Akron, OH

18-4 Sunburst
New York, c. 1845-50
Cotton, 91" x 87"

A sepia and white chintz border arranged in squares adds a sharp contrast to the center of red, green, yellow and, blue print fabric. **(C)**

Judith and James Milne
New York, NY

18-5 Sunburst
New England, c. 1850
Cotton, 47½" sq.

An unusual feature of this quilt is the chintz rose in the center of the sunburst, which is formed from solid and calico fabrics in pink, yellow, green, red, and blue. The rose motif is picked up again in the border of chintz bound in a hand-loomed tape. **(C)**

Just Us
Tucson, AZ

18-5

18-6

18-6 Sunburst
Pennsylvania (Amish), c. 1840
Cotton, 81" x 72"

Blue calico strips contain a sunburst outlined in olive-green teardrops going into rings of white, yellows, blues, and reds. In each corner are three star motifs in blues. **(C)**

Esprit De Corp
San Francisco, CA

18-7 Sunburst
Pennsylvania, c. 1860
Cotton, 92" x 90"

Shades of pinks, mauves, burgundy, and white skillfully combine to create a twinkling effect in this overall design. Note how sections have been cut out for bedposts. **(B)**

Phyllis Haders
New York, NY

19 | Log Cabins

One of the most versatile designs in quilt making is the Log Cabin, known by various pattern names depending on the manner in which the "logs" have been arranged. Basically made of squares, these patterns range from the simple to the complex. A simple pattern is "Courthouse Steps" (19-2), composed of a Square with light-colored fabrics placed on the top and bottom of each square, dark fabrics on the two sides, and a center of a contrasting color. Although the pattern is called "Courthouse Steps," the placement of the "logs" creates spool shapes. A somewhat more complicated pattern is "Barn Raising" (19-6), which is composed of squares that are divided into two triangles, one of which is pieced all in light fabrics, the other in dark; and these are joined together, making a series of narrow diamonds across the quilt (19-7) or wide diamonds covering the entire dimension of the quilt (19-8). A very busy Log Cabin variation, but one that must give great satisfaction upon completion, is "Windmill Blades," sometimes known as the "Pineapple" pattern (19-11). In this pattern, alternating "blades" of dark and light fabrics emanate from the center square of each square to the corners, increasing in width as they progress outward.

Mention should be made of a fourth pattern in the Log Cabin style, "Straight Furrow" (7-3), which is so much like "Streaks of Lightning" (7-4) that it has been placed in the Jagged Stripes category (section 7) for easy comparison.

Concluding this section are some designs (19-14, 19-15, 19-16) which, though not exactly in the style of the patterns discussed above, are nonetheless creative variations of the Log Cabin form.

Log Cabin quilts are seldom quilted because the design is held in place by the very construction of the surface, in which overlapping "logs" are stitched down on top of one another. Occasionally, Log Cabin patterns are "tufted"—that is, tied together to hold the quilt in place. Log Cabin quilts may also occasionally be framed by a plain quilted border.

19-0 Log Cabin (color plate)
New Jersey, c. 1880
Wool challis, 82" sq.

Earth tones, predominantly in solid colors, form a bulbous design in dark contrast to the lighter fabrics in this quilt. **(C)**

Tewksbury Antiques
Oldwick, NJ

19-1 Log Cabin (Courthouse Steps)
Pennsylvania (Amish), c. 1871
Cotton, 84" sq.

Prints of yellow with red dots, white with blue half-spheres, light-blue flecked with chevrons, and blue plaid contrast with darker-colored prints of reds, greens, and browns. A print of black with green vine design and small yellow buds forms the border. The back of the quilt is made of large squares of fabric used in the front design. **(B)**

Jonathan and Gail Holstein
New York, NY

19-1

19-2

19-2 Log Cabin (Courthouse Steps)
Lancaster County, Pennsylvania (Amish), c. 1860
Wool, 43" x 36"

Solid fabric of deep green makes the dark spaces of this design which
stand in contrast to the lighter calicoes and ginghams of the "spool"
shapes. **(C)**

Phyllis Haders
New York, NY

19-3 Log Cabin (Courthouse Steps)
Lancaster County, Pennsylvania (Amish), dated 1869
Wool challis, 77" x 72" sq.
Made by Mary Tice

An orange, green, and blue border frames Log Cabin blocks punctuated with prints, stripes, and solid blues with a red square in each center. **(C)**

Jonathan and Gail Holstein
New York, NY

19-4 Log Cabin (Courthouse Steps)
Pennsylvania (Amish), c. 1880
Wool challis, 90" x 84"

Burgundy, red, mauve, green, and blue are the dark colors in this design contrasted with lighter pastel colors. **(B)**

Phyllis Haders
New York, NY

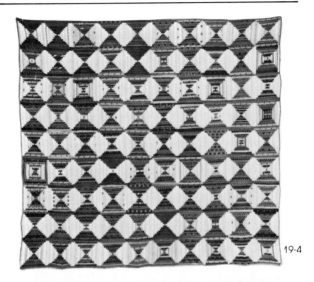

19-4

19-5

19-5 Log Cabin (Barn Raising)
Ohio (Amish), c. 1880
Wool, 76" sq.

Red, brown, grey, and plaid fabric unite clearly delineated diamonds of light and dark patterns. **(C)**

Sandra Mitchell
Southfield, MI

19-6 Log Cabin (Barn Raising)
Lewisburg, Pennsylvania (Amish), c. 1880
Silk, 68" sq.

5500 pieces comprise this light and dark design with a vivid red border. **(B)**

Smithsonian Institution
Washington, DC

19-7 Log Cabin (Barn Raising)
Pennsylvania (Amish), c. 1880
Silk, 76" sq.

Earth tones in contrast to light pinks and soft mauve make a striking light and dark effect in this quilt. **(B)**

Phyllis Haders
New York, NY

19-7

19-8

19-8 Log Cabin (Barn Raising)
Lancaster County, Pennsylvania (Mennonite), c. 1870
Wool challis, 43″ sq.

Crib quilt of earth tones with red center, framed by light-blue and beige border. **(C)**

Phyllis Haders
New York, NY

19-9 Log Cabin Variation (Barn Raising)
Kentucky (Amish), c. 1860-70
Wool, 90" x 75"

A rhythmic arrangement of reds, browns, beige, and greys placed in the square design of the Log Cabin appear in a Greek key or fret motif across the face of the quilt. **(C)**

Darwin D. Bearley
Akron, OH

19-10 Log Cabin (Light and Dark)
Lancaster County, Pennsylvania (Amish), c. 1860
Wool challis, 87" sq.

Light pinks and greens contrast with dark brown and deep purple to create this typical Log Cabin design, also known as "Sunshine and Shadow." This pattern should not be confused with the "Sunshine and Shadow" popular among the Amish. (See, for example, 8-5). **(C)**

Jonathan and Gail Holstein
New York, NY

19-10

19-11 Log Cabin (Windmill Blades)
Indiana (Amish), c. 1870
Cotton, 75" x 70"

19-11

Three sides of this quilt are in the Log Cabin design cut in half, making a sawtooth. The center section of pineapples are in blues, reds, browns, and greens with contrasting lighter prints. **(C)**

Phyllis Haders
New York, NY

19-12 Log Cabin (Windmill Blades)
Pennsylvania, c. 1880
Wool challis, 88" x 74"

The effect of spinning windmill blades is achieved by meticulous planning in the juxtaposition of fabrics. A small striped border encloses this busy design. **(C)**

Phyllis Haders
New York, NY

19-13 Log Cabin
Maine, c. 1860
Cotton, 80" sq.

These whirling windmill blades of white and grey fabric are pinned by a red square in the center. The background colors are shades of light-brown calicoes. **(C)**

Phyllis Haders
New York, NY

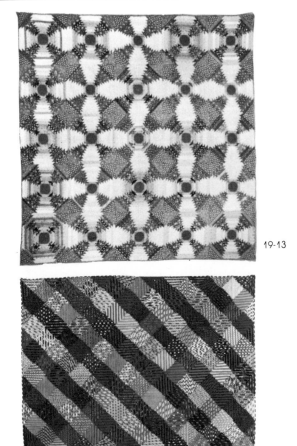

19-13

19-14

19-14 Log Cabin
Indiana, c. 1880
Wool, 72″ sq.

The multi-colored prints in this design create the illusion of rippling waves. **(B)**

Sandra Mitchell
Southfield, MI

19-15 Log Cabin
Probably Michigan, c. 1900
Silk, wool and cotton, 56″ x 37″

A crib quilt of earth tones punctuated occasionally by red is arranged in a square Log Cabin design. **(A)**

Folkways
Indianapolis, IN

19-16 Log Cabin
New Jersey, c. 1910
Cotton, 95″ x 82″

Soft yellow and brown bars form bow ties enclosed by a peach-colored picket fence with gates on each side. **(C)**

Phyllis Haders
New York, NY

20 | Hourglasses

A design whose basic form is composed of two Triangles with points touching end to end and resembling an hourglass is referred to by this common name. Designs created by joining triangular shapes into an Hourglass pattern are relatively easy to accomplish, and variety in the design is achieved by the interplay of larger and smaller shapes as well as the clever juxtaposition of fabric patterns and colors. The quilts illustrated in this section range from the simple to the complex and include such Hourglass variations as "Lady of the Lake" (20-25) and "Fox and Geese" (20-3).

20-O Hourglass (color plate)
New York, c. 1850
Silk, 32½" x 31½"

A colorful cradle quilt with a multitude of hourglass designs in a pattern called "Broken Dishes." **(B)**

Phyllis Haders
New York, NY

20-1 Hourglass
Place unknown, c. 1920
Silk, 77" sq.

Hourglass shapes in light blue and shades of yellow point in different directions within the diagonals, creating a busy design. **(A)**

Metropolitan Museum of Art
New York, NY

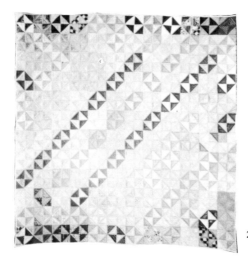

20-1

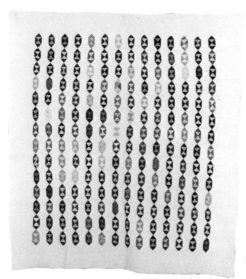

20-2

20-2 Hourglass
Ohio, c. 1870
Cotton, 82" x 79"

Light printed hourglasses are set on contrasting backgrounds against a white field quilted in hearts, birds, stars, crosses, and leaves. The white border is quilted in diamond pattern. **(A)**

Kelter-Malcé Antiques
New York, NY

20-3 Fox and Geese
Cumberland County, Pennsylvania, c. 1880
Cotton, 67" x 84"

Red, brown, and blue calicoes in hourglass shapes rest on white diamonds surrounded by a red calico background. **(A)**

Tewksbury Antiques
Oldwick, NJ

20-4 Lady of the Lake
New York, c. 1865
Cotton, 85" x 80"

Brown, red, and grey printed fabrics are employed in this pattern taken from the title of a popular poem by Sir Walter Scott. This is one of the few designs that has the same name in all sections of the country. **(A)**

Judith and James Milne
New York, NY

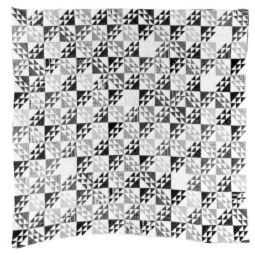

20-4

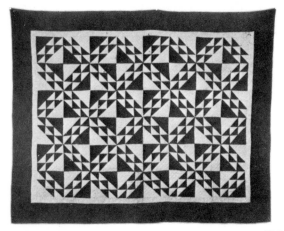

20-5

20-5 Lady of the Lake
Ohio (Amish), c. 1925
Cotton, 75" x 70"

Black and cranberry-red hourglasses are the center design in squares
made by small triangles. A black border and narrow tape of red frame
this quilt. **(B)**

Darwin D. Bearley
Akron, OH

20-6 Hourglass and Bow Tie
Fowlerville, MI, c. 1890
Cotton, 78" x 70"

Each square of the Hourglass motif has a bow tie on the bottom of the square except for the second square from the left of the top row. There is no bow tie at the bottom of this square because the hourglasses have been placed differently, starting in the upper left with a vertical hourglass rather than a horizontal, changing the whole design ever so subtly. **(A)**

Sandra Mitchell
Southfield, MI

21 | Bow Ties

The Bow Tie pattern is great fun because it creates optical illusions, the effects of which lie truly in the eye of the beholder. Sometimes the Bow Tie design appears as a solid color (21-1), or it can be viewed as bows of one color with the tie or knot in a contrasting color (21-2). The Bow Tie can be very easily distinguished from the Hourglass: It usually has a pouchy or arrow-shaped bow and a very definite knot, whereas the Hourglass consists of two Triangles joined at their apexes to form a shape resembling an Hourglass.

21-O Bow Tie (color plate)
Ohio (Amish), c. 1930
Cotton, 84" x 73"

Rows of arrow-shaped bow ties are held in place by brick colored hexagons which, in turn, become pouchy bow ties when viewed on the diagonal. Note the white bow tie in the upper right corner. A minute quilted vine and leaf motif is in the mauve frame while a running feather quilting and small hearts are located in the dark border. **(C)**

Esprit De Corp
San Francisco, CA

21-1 Bow Tie
Probably Tennessee, c. 1890
Cotton, 86" x 80"

Since the Bow Tie pattern frequently creates an optical illusion, this quilt may be seen as blue bows on a white background or as white ties with blue knots. Note the quilter's inability to turn the corner on the lower left and upper right. **(A)**

Goose Tracks Antiques
Knoxville, TN

21-2 Bow Tie
Holmes County, Ohio (Amish), c. 1910
Cotton, 83" x 66"

A raspberry border edged in indigo frames a square of indigo with lighter blue, various shades of raspberry making up bow ties and the pastel square in center. Notice one white bow tie in center, top row. Feather quilting and small stars in border. **(B)**

Esprit De Corp
San Francisco, CA

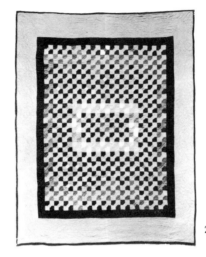

21-2

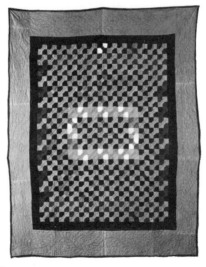

21-3

21-3 Bow Tie
Pennsylvania (Amish), c. 1900
Wool and cotton, 80" x 66"

Rust and black with center in contrasting lighter shades of rose and green hand-dyed textiles. Again the white bow tie is visible at the top. (See 21-2.) Feather and star quilting around the border. **(C)**

Just Us
Tucson, AZ

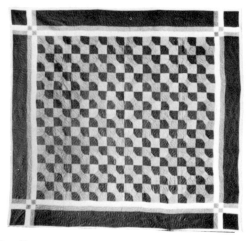

21-4 Bow Tie
Ohio, c. 1915-20
Polished cotton and satin, 80" x 72"

Raspberry and midnight blue combine to create crossed bow ties in each square: One is in a solid shade, the other has dark bows and a light knot. Light yellow and raspberry-colored bars frame the design and extend to the four corners anchored in place by a four patch. Beautiful feather quilting meanders around the deep-blue border. **(C)**

Collection of Barbara S. Janos and Barbara Ross
New York, NY

21-5 Bow Tie
Ohio, c. 1910
Cotton, 88" x 72"

Black ties on red diamonds, green ties on orange diamonds, and blue ties on brown diamonds are framed in black with a green border. **(B)**

21-6 Bow Tie
Place unknown, c. 1900
Cotton, 84" x 76"

Puffy white bow ties with a deep-blue knot rest against a red background framed with a red, white, and blue sawtooth border. **(A)**

22 | Pinwheels

The Pinwheel design, as its name suggests, attempts to simulate the blades of a whirring pinwheel. It is also frequently referred to as a Swastika, a very ancient symbol of good fortune, health, and prosperity. Often used in medieval decoration and embroidery, the Pinwheel or Swastika motif was a common device in American Indian art and in Colonial architecture, an occurrence that might possibly have served as a design influence on early quilters.

This four-pronged or four-footed design is illustrated in a variety of ways in the pages that follow—from a true Pinwheel, found in color plate 22, or the "Rolling Star" design (22-1), to a free interpretation of the symbol that suggests a kaleidoscope (22-5) or the Pinwheels evolving from the "Melon" pattern (22-4).

As one might expect, this blade design is known by many popular pattern names, chief among them "Windmill," "Waterwheel," and "Millwheel." It is easy to understand how these "Wheel" patterns, based on machinery so necessary for 19th-century life, became sources for quilt designs whose form derives from the simple Four Patch construction.

22-0 Pinwheel (color plate)
Grand Rapids, Michigan, c. 1875
Cotton, 78" x 76"

Grand Rapids Flour Company sacks have been used as backing for this quilt that features patriotically-colored pinwheels that rest on grey squares. **(C)**

Smith, Hinchman & Grylls Associates, Inc.
Detroit, MI

22-1 Pinwheel
Place unknown, c. 1820
Cotton, 107" x 85"

Elegant chintzes combined with more subdued calicoes make up this complicated design whose predominant motif is the pinwheel, although it is sometimes called "Rolling Star." **(C)**

Smithsonian Institution
Washington, DC

22-2 Pinwheels and Mosaic
Place unknown, c. 1850
Silk, 84" x 82"

Large pinwheels are of nutmeg, rust, chocolate brown, lemon yellow, moss green, and accents of navy blue. Small pinwheel border of deep mauve forms transition of colors from large pinwheels to the border of squares in light mauves, blacks, and light greens. The mosaic center is filled with blue, beige, and café-au-lait hexagons. **(C)**

Esprit De Corp
San Francisco, CA

22-3 Pinwheel
Ohio (Amish), c. 1900
Cotton, 88" x 71"

Pinwheels developed from a four patch are of indigo and light shades of pinkish white with an indigo frame and tan border of clam-shell quilting. Whorl and diamond quilting are found in the white sections of the center design. **(B)**

Esprit De Corp
San Francisco, CA

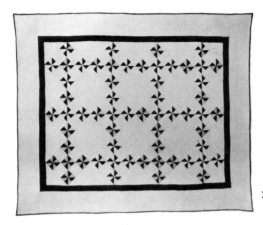

22-3

22-4 Watermelon
New Jersey, c. 1880
Cotton, 78" x 72"

This changing pinwheel design of
green and orange melon shapes
and squares sometimes appears
as melons in a circle. **(A)**

Tewksbury Antiques
Oldwick, NJ

22-5

22-5 Pinwheel
Ohio (Amish), c. 1920
Cotton, 69" x 46"

Black pinwheels connected by a white square are set against a kaleidoscope of pinks, greens, mauves, and purples, all framed in a black border. **(B)**

Kelter-Malcé Antiques
New York, NY

22-6 Pinwheel
Indiana (Amish), c. 1890
Cotton, 82" x 69"

A handsome quilt composed of blue, green, black, beige, and purple pinwheels on contrasting diamonds framed with red bars anchored in each corner with a beige diamond. A deep navy-blue border surrounds the whole design. **(B)**

22-7 Windmill
New England, c. 1860
Cotton, 84" x 96"

Triangles of light and dark fabric are joined to create a windmill effect. The entire design is quilted in the herringbone pattern. **(B)**

23 | Drunkard's Path

Upon viewing a quilt in the Drunkard's Path pattern, the eye immediately perceives the irregular lines—the "crooked road" that every Victorian moralist knew led unmistakably to hell. The design is generally done in only two colors, one light and one dark, joined together in a design that very much suggests 19th-century paper cutouts.

Certainly no prospective bride would want a design depicting the meandering irregular path of a drunkard as part of her dowry quilts, yet this interesting design might well have become acceptable to a bride when known as "Pumpkin Vine," "Country Husband," "Solomon's Puzzle" (the Amish name for this pattern), "Robbing Peter to Pay Paul" (see 14-5 for another version of this pattern name), and "Rocky Road to Dublin" (a name which after the Gold Rush appeared as "Rocky Road to California").

Once begun, this pattern is not particularly difficult to execute and creates a handsome design—in spite of its name—when completed.

23-0 Drunkard's Path (color plate)
Pennsylvania (Amish), c. 1880
Calico, 84" sq.

The zigzag pattern in this quilt is firmly confined by the double red lines forming the border.

Phyllis Haders
New York, NY

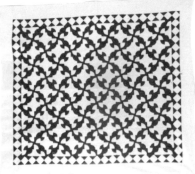

23-1 Drunkard's Path
Ohio (Amish), c. 1890
Cotton, 75" x 50"

This handsome black and white design is framed in small diamonds and a large white border. **(B)**

Darwin D. Bearley
Akron, OH

23-2 Drunkard's Path
Ohio (Amish), c. 1925
Cotton, 75" sq.

Quilted crosses hold each of these irregular shapes in place. The deep dusty rose of the design makes a handsome contrast to the black background. **(B)**

Darwin D. Bearley
Akron, OH

23-3 Drunkard's Path
Ohio, c. 1930
Cotton, 84" sq.

This very popular and typical design is enhanced by the use of a white Drunkard's Path pattern against a deep green background. Alternating frames of green and white give a handsome border to this design. **(A)**

23-4 Indiana Puzzle
Indiana, c. 1920
Cotton, 86" x 72"

A little more angular than the Drunkard's Path, but employing the same basic design, this quilt is done in rose against a white field. Each corner of the border contains a Nine-Patch motif in the same colors as the center. Clam-shell quilting gives depth to the main design, and the sides of the quilt are done in a double-rope motif. **(B)**

24 | Baskets

Long before contemporary trendsetters and the Sunday supplements rediscovered the joys of country living and embalmed the humble basket as a work of art, the common basket served a most useful function. It was used on the homestead to gather eggs, fruit, wine, and cider; for recreation on fishing trips and picnic lunches; and in everyday activities for laundry, marketing, measuring, and sewing. For the American quilter, the most important basket of all was the scrap basket—for fabrics, not for trash.

It is not surprising, therefore, to find the Basket design a prevalent one in pieced work as well as in appliquéd design. The pieced basket pattern is virtually always the same design—small triangular-shaped fabrics joined in the form of an anvil to which may or may not be attached a handle. Sometimes the handles create a design motif of their own (24-8), or they may appear to be as prominent as the basket itself (24-5). Frequently done in only two colors, blue or red and white, these baskets are a geometrically-conceived abstract interpretation of an important and useful household item.

24-O Baskets (color plate)
New York, c. 1865
Cotton, 89" x 80"

These sprightly baskets in calico, gingham, and chintz cut in anvil
shapes have looped handles whose design is repeated by clam-shell
quilting in the white background. **(B)**

Judith and James Milne
New York, NY

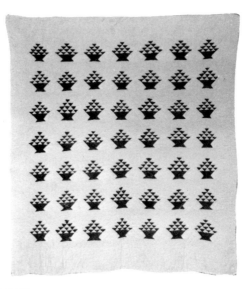

24-1 Baskets
Ohio, c. 1880
Cotton, 38" x 37"

Typical of quilts in this pattern, this crib quilt is in blue and white with a
pyramid of triangles atop an anvil-shaped basket. **(C)**

Jay Johnson
New York, NY

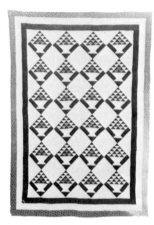

24-2 Baskets
Indiana, c. 1885
Cotton, 100" x 72"

This red, white, and blue flower basket design is set on a white background interspersed with wreath and cube quilting. **(B)**

Private Collection

24-3 Basket of Chips
Michigan, c. 1900
Cotton, 80" x 75"

A red grid pinned in place by white squares, with green baskets of red triangles on white background, framed in a red and white border. **(B)**

Darwin D. Bearley
Akron, OH

24-4 Basket of Flowers
New Jersey, dated 1855
Cotton, 95¾" x 84¾"

24-4

A red lattice grid separates green baskets appliquéd with orange triangles. On the white background around each basket are a variety of
quilted designs, with a heart under every basket. Green triangles,
which rest on an orange background, fill the space along the edge of
the grid. This quilt is initialed in two baskets in the top row, and the
place of origin and date appear in two baskets on the bottom. **(C)**

New Jersey State Museum
Trenton, NJ

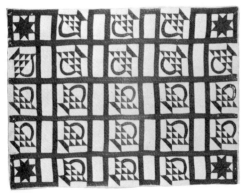

24-5

24-5 Baskets
Connecticut, c. 1870
Cotton, 44" x 33"

A cradle quilt consists of red and white baskets separated by a grid of single vertical and double horizontal bars, anchored in each corner of an eight-pointed star. **(C)**

Phyllis Haders
New York, NY

24-6 Baskets
New Jersey, c. 1840
Cotton, 84" sq.

Red and white pieced baskets rest in a double frame of white diamonds on red. Double-edged diagonal quilting is along the border, while the center is filled with vertical quilting and stuffed pumpkin seed design between each basket. **(D)**

Tewksbury Antiques
Oldwick, NJ

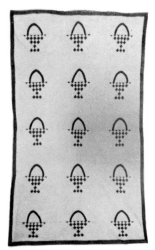

24-7 Baskets
Indiana, c. 1885
Cotton, 94" x 64"

Indigo and white baskets, appliquéd handles, with wreath quilting between baskets, and diamond quilting around baskets. **(B)**

Private Collection

24-8 Baskets
Ohio, c. 1890
Cotton, 78" x 74"

Interlocking handles unite this design which usually is conceived of
as separate elements. Indigo
pieces against a white background are placed in a dark
frame with white border. Baskets
are quilted in each of the handles
of the design. **(B)**

Judith and James Milne
New York, NY

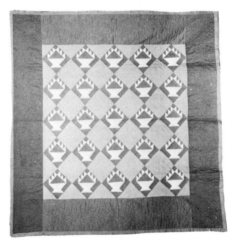

24-9 Baskets
Pennsylvania (Amish), c. 1910
Wool, 84" sq.

White baskets sit on red squares placed on a turquoise background
framed in turkey red. There is clam-shell quilting on the baskets, whorl
motifs in the turquoise squares, and running feather motifs around the
border. **(C)**

Phyllis Haders
New York, NY

24-10 Baskets
Iowa, c. 1880
Cotton, 86" x 78"

Fifty-six pieced baskets in red and white and blue and white are filled with different varieties of flowers and placed on white diamonds that alternate with diamonds of the dark background color. **(C)**

24-11 Baskets
North Carolina, c. 1830
Cotton, 86" sq.

One hundred and fifty-six minute baskets in the typical blue and white pieced design (24-1) cover the center of this quilt, yet leave enough space for a narrow sawtooth border. Half of the baskets face left, and the other half right. **(C)**

25 | Fans

Oriental motifs, among them the Fan, have had a marked influence on American design since Colonial times. But, in part inspired by the popularity of the Japanese Pavilion at the 1876 Centennial Exhibition in Philadelphia, the late-Victorian period enjoyed a particularly revitalized appreciation of things Oriental. Women of the day, of course, used fans as a practical and fashionable accessory, and paper fans, emblazoned with a commercial message, were a commonplace of Victorian advertising.

As an artistic component of quilts, the Fan shape lends itself to a variety of alternatives. It can be seen completely extended (color plate 25), half opened (25-1), or nicely filling a corner space (25-1). Sometimes Fans can be treated in a very simple, straightforward manner, with the shape appearing in only two colors and the background becoming an integral part of the design (25-2). Fan designs frequently appear in Crazy quilts (40-7), where they are composed of many different fabrics that complement the jumbled aspect of these quilts.

25-O Fans (color plate)
Indiana, c. 1920
Wool, 90" x 81"

A sophisticated sense of design is evident in this quilt. Although appearing as rows of interlocking fans, every square has a separate fan in one corner, and the placement of the fans within the square has been methodically thought out to construct a linear design. **(C)**

Phyllis Haders
New York, NY

25-1 Fans
Probably Michigan, c. 1905
Cotton, 86″ x 76″
Made by Minna Stienke

Colors on the somber side of the palette, punctuated with a few plaids and calicoes, are snippets of clothing belonging to the quilter and her husband during the first year of their marriage. **(B)**

Mayeve Tate
Princeton, NJ

25-2 Fans
Lancaster County, Pennsylvania, c. 1920
Cotton, 72″ x 66″

Strips of indigo are spaced to incorporate the beige background as part of the fan design. **(A)**

Security Pacific National Bank Collection
San Francisco, CA

25-3 Fans
Pennsylvania, c. 1930
Cotton, 76″ x 71″

Gaily-colored calicoes, plaids, and ginghams make up the fans placed in the lower left corner of the white squares that form the background of this design. Each fan has a bright red center. **(A)**

25-4 Fans
New York, c. 1930
Cotton, 82" sq.

A patriotic-appearing quilt; red and blue striped fans opened about two-thirds of the way make a repetitious design across the face of the quilt which is framed by a red bar at the top and bottom and a blue bar on the sides. **(A)**

25-5 Fans
Pennsylvania, c. 1930
Cotton, 86" x 73"

Pieced fans in bright calicoes with red centers are placed in rows against an orange background framed with a red border. **(A)**

26 | Trees

The tree represented on the pieced quilts illustrated in this section is the pine, which had special significance for early settlers. To them it was an essential of life, for pine trees became their very homes and furniture and were used as a symbol on their coins, flags, and documents. In their quilts this pattern represented loyalty and steadfastness. The basic form of the design is the same in all areas of the country—a geometric shape composed of small triangles with a solid-colored trunk. Although the trees are most frequently arranged in horizontal or vertical rows, they are occasionally placed on the diagonal, either with or without a grid, and they generally appear in only two colors—red, blue, or green on a white field. The "Pine Tree" pattern is also known as "Temperance Tree," "Tree of Paradise," and "Tall Pine Tree."

26-0 Trees (color plate)
Indiana, c. 1890
Cotton, 86" x 80"

The dark lattice grid emphasizes the geometric form of the trees. As is frequent in this pattern, half of the trees point in one direction while the other half head in the opposite direction. **(C)**

Sandra Mitchell
Southfield, MI

26-1 Pine Trees
Ohio, c. 1870
Cotton, 80" x 66"

26-1

Red leaves and moss-green stems in the shape of arrows create a geometric pattern framed with a red and white border. **(B)**

Judith and James Milne
New York, NY

26-2

26-2 Tree of Life
Ohio (Amish), dated May 2, 1921
Cotton, 77" sq.

Black and moss-green trees on white; feather circle quilted in each black diamond; feather quilting around the border. **(B)**

Esprit De Corp
San Francisco, CA

26-3 Trees of Paradise
Indiana, c. 1840
Cotton, 84" sq.

A typical pieced tree design done in red and green has trunks that appear like large spades. A variety of quilting techniques give depth to the white background. **(B)**

27 | Alphabets and Letters

As a teaching tool, the pieced quilt was unique. From it a child could learn sewing, geometry, graphic design, perspective, and color. But if he was fortunate enough to have an Alphabet quilt, he could learn as well his numbers and letters. In addition to those quilts that are composed of the letters of the alphabet, some quilts contain only one letter as a design motif or may consist of Biblical quotations, prayers, or well-known sayings of the day. The Lord's Prayer was a particular favorite.

Arranging the alphabet to fit a square or grid pattern presents an interesting design problem since the twenty-six letters do not fit into any easily divisible number of squares. The quilters arrived at a series of ingenious solutions to this problem—dropping the "Z" altogether, placing it in one of the four corners of the quilt (27-2), or letting it begin a new row that was supplemented with numbers or a date (27-1).

27-0 Alphabet (color plate)
Pennsylvania, c. 1890
Cotton, 88" x 82"

The way this alphabet has been laid out there is no room for the "Z," which does not appear. The "G" seems to lack a tail, and it takes a hard look to be certain that the "E" is not a "D." **(C)**

Kelter-Malcé Antiques
New York, NY

27-1 Alphabet
Probably New York, dated 1896
Cotton, 96" x 84"
Made by Elva Smith

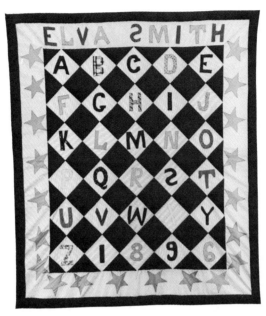

27-1

The maker reversed the "S" in her name and was consistent by re-
versing the "S" in the alphabet. By incorporating the date into the design, the quilter solved the problem of twenty-six letters in the alphabet
not making an even number of rows. **(D)**

Private Collection

27-2 Alphabet
Berks County, Pennsylvania, c. 1875
Cotton, 80" sq.

Because the twenty-sixth letter of the alphabet is the lone hold-out in
the pattern of five rows of five letters each, it has been placed in the
left-hand corner as a solution to the problem of creating a symmetrical
design. **(D)**

Private Collection

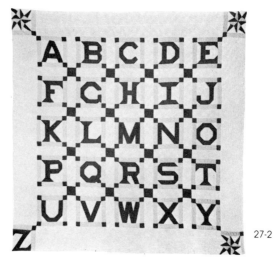

27-2

27-3 Letter "D"
Place unknown, c. 1880
Cotton, 85" x 80"

A single initial can make a very impressive quilt. In this case a rectangularly-conceived letter "D" in white is set on squares of red and blue triangles. A white grid divides the letters. **(B)**

28 | Yo-Yos and Puffs

As in every art form, someone has to create the unusual; and in the realm of quilts there are at least two special kinds—the Yo-Yo and the Puff—that are slightly different in technique from either the conventional pieced or appliquéd quilt. Because Yo-Yo and Puff quilts are visually and constructionally related to pieced work, they have been included in this guide at the very end of the section devoted to the pieced quilt.

The Yo-Yo, known also as "Bon-Bon" or "Popcorn" (color plate 28), is made of small pieces of fabric formed into rosettes which are in turn pieced together into a top. Since they do not have a backing and are not quilted, they are light in weight and are best used as a summer spread.

On the other hand, the Puff (28-3) is heavier than the Yo-Yo since the small squares from which it is made are stuffed, and the entire quilt is backed. Like the Yo-Yo, however, the Puff is not quilted. Thus, both the Yo-Yo and the Puff are made from bits of fabric, pieced together in rows, and are not quilted.

28-0 Yo-Yo or Popcorn (color plate)
Massachusetts, c. 1890
Silk, 64" x 58"

Because the majority of its little circles are white, this quilt suggests the appearance of popcorn balls bouncing around the design. A rich red silk border frames the energetic center. **(B)**

Judith and James Milne
New York, NY

28-1 Yo-Yo (detail)
Missouri, c. 1920
Cotton, quilt 78" sq.

Small scraps of fabric pulled together in the middle resemble miniature berets or tam-o'-shanters. **(A)**

Private Collection

28-2 Yo-Yo (detail)
North Carolina, c. 1900
Wool, quilt 86" sq.

28-2

The typical Yo-Yo quilt was not very warm since it had no backing. However, one done in wool (as seen here) would make good sense. **(A)**

Private Collection

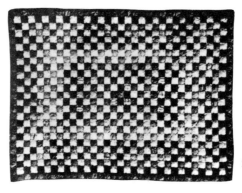

28-3

28-3 Puffs
Missouri, c. 1890
Silk, 86" x 80"

This type of quilt is made by assembling together small squares of brightly colored silk that have been backed in muslin and stuffed. It is similar to the Yo-Yo in the use of a great variety of small motifs joined in rows; however, this pattern has a backing where the Yo-Yo does not. **(A)**

Private Collection

28-4 Puffs
Maine, c. 1875
Wool, 76" x 70"

Red, black, yellow, and plaids in these colors, are made into puffs which are joined together like a One-Patch design. Made of wool, this quilt must have been a welcome cover on a cold night in Maine. **(A)**

II | Appliquéd Quilts

The design configurations of appliquéd quilts are far easier to understand than those of pieced quilts, for they are mainly drawn from nature and are more or less realistically represented.

As its name implies, the appliquéd quilt is made of fabric cut into shapes that are generally larger than those used in piece work; these shapes, as in the pieced quilt, are applied to a background. Many appliquéd quilts are not in fact quilted, but were used as tops or summer spreads, particularly in the South where warmth from the quilt was not a prime necessity.

Because appliquéd quilts are not based on design motifs that develop one from the other—as in the geometric forms of pieced quilts—they are organized in this guide according to the most prevalent forms of the natural world that they seek to simulate—Flowers, Trees, Leaves, Birds, Fruit, etc.

The most profuse designs in appliqué are the many delightful Flowers which in this guide have been divided into three sections for ease of identification. In section 30 are to be found quilts appliquéd with only flowers, whereas section 31 covers quilts of floral designs placed in such containers as baskets and flower pots. The third section (32) includes quilts decorated with wreaths of flowers in various designs.

Although the sections devoted to Leaves, Feathers, Birds, and Fruit are self-explanatory, an additional word is perhaps necessary about the category on Buildings (35). Buildings are not, of course, aspects of the natural world, but no one can deny their imposing presence in the natural landscape or their importance as a design motif in fancywork. The house that had its place in needlework samplers of the 18th and early 19th centuries was easily transposed to the appliquéd and pieced quilts of the Victorian era.

The final categories of this part of the book represent special uses to which the appliqué technique can be put. Many Presentation quilts (section 41) are, of course, made up of appliquéd blocks as are the star-spangled Patriotic quilts (section 42) so highly prized today. Hawaiian quilts (section 39) and Crazy quilts (section 40) present us with a uniqueness that is discussed in their respective sections.

The superb appliquéd quilt illustrated in color plate II (p. 36) can readily serve as a "sampler" of appliqué designs. Incorporating such motifs as Flowers, Fruit, Baskets, Birds, and Patriotic symbols, this Presentation quilt was made of cotton in either New York or New Jersey in the late 19th century, measures 78 inches by 66 inches, and is reproduced with the permission of Just Us, Tucson, Arizona. A schematic drawing of the quilt appears on the following page together with identifications of the designs that make up its component parts.

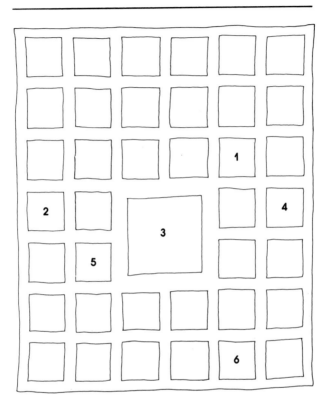

1. Flowers
2. Fruit
3. Birds
4. Patriotic
5. Flowers in Containers
6. Leaves

29 | Chintz Appliqué

Early chintz fabric was so very expensive and highly prized that as it wore out individual motifs were saved and arranged artistically on white backgrounds (color plate 29). This technique of placing used chintz on a solid background originated in France and was called **Broderie Perse** (Persian Embroidery). In **Broderie Perse** and its American counterpart, there are at least three forms of design. One features a central "Tree of Life" motif (color plate 29); another applies the cut-out chintz informally on the background (29-3); and the third is arranged in a framed center pattern (29-4).

In Chintz Appliqué the scraps of fabric may be arranged in loosely-composed designs (29-3) or in tightly-constructed geometric patterns (29-2). Chintz counterpanes are quite large in size since they were generally made for huge four-poster beds that were particularly prevalent in the South well into the 19th century.

29-0 Chintz (Tree of Life) (color plate)
Pennsylvania, c. 1830
Chintz and cotton, 106" x 104"
Made by Mrs. Benjamin Mumford

Resembling a Persian garden, this design, inspired by oriental rugs so prominent in interiors of the period, is a beautifully executed Broderie Perse. **(D)**

Detroit Historical Museum
Detroit, MI

29-1 Chintz (detail)
Pennsylvania, c. 1830
Chintz and cotton, Quilt
106" x 104"
Made by Mrs. Benjamin Mumford

This detail of color plate 29, from a branch in the lower left-hand corner section of the quilt, shows the variety of motifs comprising this beautiful chintz.

Detroit Historical Museum
Detroit, MI

29-2 Chintz
Connecticut, c. 1840
Cotton, 98" x 91"

Sprigs of roses fill the center ground, which is framed by a larger interpretation of the rose motif surrounded by a running pink leaf border. **(C)**

Phyllis Haders
New York, NY

29-2

29-3

29-3 Chintz
Pennsylvania or Ohio, c. 1845
Cotton, 38″ x 34″

A floral central medallion is harmoniously balanced by three pheasants on top and bottom and two smaller birds at each side. The birds rest on floral chintz, repeating the center motif. A very pointed sawtooth border frames the design. **(D)**

Private Collection

29-4 Chintz
Washington, D.C., c. 1834-38
Cotton and chintz, 114" x 109"
Made by Mrs. James Lusby

Flower, bird and butterfly motifs are cut from chintz and appliquéd to a white cotton background. **(D)**

Smithsonian Institution
Washington, DC

29-5 Chintz
Savannah, Georgia, dated 1824
Cotton, 92" sq.

Appliquéd floral tree of green, pink, yellow, and brown roses and leaves with zigzag border of red, green, yellow, and blue floral chintz on white background of cube and diagonal quilting. **(D)**

Private Collection

29-5

29-6

29-6 Chintz
Probably New England, c. 1837
Cotton, 106" sq.

Stars form a spread horseshoe above the head of the eagle who looks to the sheaf of arrows in his right talons. A variety of chintzes form contrasting swag and sawtooth borders placed on a white background filled with elaborate trapunto leaves, grape clusters, floral motifs and thimble quilting. **(E)**

Private Collection

30 | Flowers

By far the most profuse design in appliquéd quilts is the floral motif. Even just the mention of an appliquéd quilt immediately brings to mind a white quilt filled with colorful flowers. Of these flower patterns, the Rose is the favorite. Almost every bride-to-be, once her betrothal was announced, began work on her bridal quilt, the last of her thirteen dowry quilts which was usually in the "Rose of Sharon" pattern (30-4). This quilt was often reserved for use upon special occasions or was placed on a bed in the guest room. Many states or regions of the country have rose patterns named after them, as in the "Prairie Rose" and "Dixie Rose" and as in the roses named for the states of Ohio, Indiana, Kentucky, and California. Just about all of these quilts are done in red, yellow, and green, with pink being used occasionally for buds. A special combination of colors, however, occurs in 30-5, where teal, blue, and brown are used to good effect.

Next in popularity is the Tulip which can closely resemble the real flower (30-9) or may be more abstract or geometric in design (30-16 and 30-17). The flower design in 30-18 called a Lily illustrates how the same shape is used interchangeably for both the lily and the tulip. Other flower motifs include the poppy (30-22) and the coxcomb (30-20), as well as others that can only be called flowers of the imagination (30-24 and 30-25).

30-0 Whig Rose (color plate)
Connecticut, 1860
Cotton, 92" x 90"

This popular rose pattern is difficult to distinguish from the Rose of Sharon (30-5). To some extent the Whig Rose seems to have long, straight stems compared to the more bent design of the Rose of Sharon. During the 1840s two appliqué patterns, the "Whig Rose" and "Democrat Rose" appeared, deriving their names from a dispute between two political parties, the Whigs and the Democrats. **(C)**

Phyllis Haders
New York, NY

30-1 Whig Rose
Pennsylvania, c. 1880
Cotton, 76" sq.

Three rows of large red rose motifs are set among smaller pink and red rosettes with tan leaves and stems. A serpentine vine border encloses the design. **(C)**

Stella Rubin
Darnestown, MD

30-1

30-2

30-2 Whig Rose Variation
Ohio, c. 1860
Cotton, 88" sq.

A very symmetrical floral center in reds, yellows, and greens is framed by a red square. Then the center motif is picked up in a more sprightly border with flowers and berries placed in small green urns. **(C)**

Stella Rubin
Darnestown, MD

30-3 Rose of Sharon
Probably Kentucky, c. 1880
Cotton, 80" sq.

This summer top has a busy design with many stems filled with pink and red buds meandering over the surface. Four circles hold the design in place. **(A)**

Folkways
Indianapolis, IN

30-4 Rose of Sharon
Pennsylvania, c. 1857
Cotton, 92" x 88"

A vine of tulips gracefully encircles a cluster of four rose bouquets, all of the same solid fabric except for the upper left one, which is flecked. This design is also known as "California Rose." **(C)**

Just Us
Tucson, AZ

30-5 Rose of Sharon
Michigan, c. 1870
Cotton, 60" sq.

An unusual color combination of teal, blue, and brown is used in this typical Rose of Sharon pattern with a rosebud and vine border on a white field of straight line and feather quilting. **(C)**

George Kiberd
Ferndale, MI

30-6 Rose of Sharon
Indiana, c. 1885
Cotton, 88" x 70"

Red roses of Sharon with yellow centers and green leaves are surrounded by bow-knots on a serpentine border. The background is white with diagonal-line quilting. **(C)**

Private Collection

30-7 Rose of Sharon Variation
Pennsylvania, c. 1850
Cotton, 94" x 74"

Mustard-yellow centers with green bud-and-leaves designs rest on a white field broken by a red and white chintz grid surrounded by a solid red zigzag. A variety of design inconsistencies gives a playful note to this quilt. The flowers in the left-hand column reach downward while flowers in the next two columns point to the top. There is no pattern to the direction of the bud motifs in each corner of the grid, and the zigzag border breaks in several places. **(C)**

Tewksbury Antiques
Oldwick, NJ

30-7

30-8

30-8 Roses
New York, c. 1880
Cotton, 82" x 78"

Stuffed red roses with green stems and olive-colored leaves are encircled with beautiful whorl quilting. Note that there are no full-blown
roses on the center bouquet. A very simple vine border meanders
around three sides of the quilt. **(C)**

Mr. and Mrs. Robert J. Bonner
Malone, NY

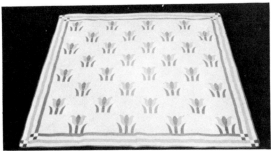

30-9 Tulip
Ann Arbor, Michigan, c. 1900
Cotton, 89" sq.
Made by Minna Stienke

The use of lavender, not ordinarily seen in Tulip quilts, is effectingly employed in a deep shade for the flower center surrounded by lighter lavender petals. The abruptly cut-off dark-green leaves appear to be growing out of the quilt. Strips of lavender, anchored by small green Four Patches, line the border. **(B)**

Mayeve Tate
Princeton, NJ

30-10 Tulip
Somerset County, Kentucky,
**   c. 1860**
Cotton, 93" x 69"

The center petal of the tulips is red; the other two are green with a green stem and leaves. **(B)**

Smithsonian Institution
Washington, DC

30-11 Tulips
Michigan, c. 1875
Cotton, 78" x 70"

Red, green, and yellow calicoes form the tulip heads of this compact

30-11

floral design. A repeat of the calico pattern is used in the sawtooth border. **(B)**

Sandra Mitchell
Southfield, MI

30-12 Tulip
Pennsylvania, c. 1870
Cotton, 82" x 70"

Four golden tulips with reddish-brown centers and green leaves grow out of a green center circle on which rests a white and reddish-brown star. This pattern repeats on a white background with simple running-stitch quilting. **(B)**

Sandra Mitchell
Southfield, MI

30-13 Tulip
Place unknown, c. 1855-65
Cotton, 78¼" x 78"

Soft coral tulips are accented by dark-green leaves and stems with each cluster of flowers joined by a green cross. The green and white diaper-pattern border is set against a coral field. There is some machine stitching on this quilt. **(C)**

Smithsonian Institution
Washington, DC

30-13

30-14 Tulip
Ohio, c. 1850
Cotton, 82" x 86"

This staid balanced design of red flowers and clear green leaves is given motion by the placement of the red triangles forming windmill blades ready to spin. Reinforcing this movement is the star motif in the center of each square. A red, white, and green border anchors the design. **(C)**

Merry Silber
Birmingham, MI

30-15 Tulip
Lebanon County, Pennsylvania, dated 1857
Cotton, 102" x 88"

Calico red tulips with mustard centers and rosette buds on green stems. A scalloped border of green entwined with more tulips. Initials "M.R." and date appear in two corners of the quilt. **(C)**

Kiracofe and Kile
San Francisco, CA

30-15

30-16 Tulip Variation
Vermont, c. 1885
Cotton, 92" x 74"

Red silhouettes of tulips perch on
tan leaves and stems surrounded
by a tulip vine in the same colors.
Small red balls, playfully placed in
the white spaces, give movement
to this rather staid design. **(C)**

Mr. and Mrs. Robert J. Bonner
Malone, NY

30-17 Tulip
Place unknown, c. 1880
Cotton, 78" sq.

Geometric tulips of mustard-yellow and red petals are supported by
green stems and leaves. Swags of green are pinned in place by red
tassels and bows. **(C)**

Detroit Historical Museum
Detroit, MI

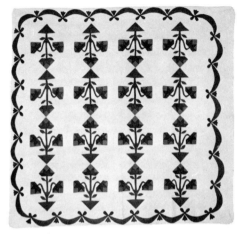

30-17

30-18

30-18 Tulip (Scripture or Bible)
Pennsylvania, c. 1845
Cotton, 102″ x 100″

A blue-green chintz border surrounds red calico flowers and spring-green diamonds. Most of the leaves are light to dark shades of green while a few have red calico stems. Near the stems of many of the flowers are quotations from the Bible—hence the name "Scripture" or "Bible" quilt. The flower in this design is sometimes referred to as a lily.
(C)

Phyllis Haders
New York, NY

30-19 Peony
Knox County, Tennessee, c. 1910
Cotton, 83" x 67"

Coral blossoms with dark centers and green leaves "grow" from the corner of each square; the squares are framed by a matching coral grid, anchored at the crossbars with a light-colored square. **(B)**

Goose Tracks Antiques
Knoxville, TN

30-20 Peony
Pennsylvania, c. 1880
Cotton, 80" x 72"

Red centers of flower are offset by the deep green leaves and stem against a background of white with diagonal line quilting while a solid grid reinforces the simple design. **(B)**

Private Collection

30-21 Peony
Ohio, c. 1890
Cotton, 80" sq.

30-21

Bright green, yellow, and red flowers sit on a white field with cube and feather quilting enclosed by a meandering vine border. **(C)**

Private Collection

30-22

30-22 Poppy
Place unknown, c. 1860
Cotton, 95″ sq.

A clean crispness of design is achieved through vivid red flowers and bright green leaves set against a white field enclosed by a small red sawtooth border. Gay sprigs of green leaves with red buds float around the border which repeats the red sawtooth motif. **(C)**

Smithsonian Institution
Washington, DC

30-23

30-23 Currants and Coxcomb
Place unknown, c. 1870
Cotton, 80" sq.

Putty-colored coxcombs with red tops and centers rotate with sprigs of currants. **(B)**

Folkways
Indianapolis, IN

30-24 Flowers
Pennsylvania, dated 1849
Cotton, 93½" x 91½"
Made by Jane Barr

Four rows, each containing four bouquets of red flowers with green pinwheel leaves, are symmetrically spaced on a white field with the quiltmaker's name and the date in stuffed work. A serpentine vine, leaf, and flower border gracefully surrounds the center design. **(C)**

Smithsonian Institution
Washington, DC

30-24

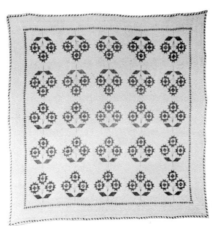

30-25

30-25 Flowers
Ohio, c. 1840
Cotton, 88" sq.

Small rosette flowers with green leaves and stem are repeated on a white background with trapunto. Two fine sawtooth edges frame the design and outline the border. **(C)**

Phyllis Haders
New York, NY

31 | Flowers in Containers

An interesting variety of containers were combined with flowers in appliquéd quilts, and in the following pages are to be found some of the basic types used. A favorite seems to have been the basket, which could be used as an important design element—as in color plate 31 and in 31-1—or might be hardly noticeable at all—as in the very busy floral pattern depicted in 31-4. Baskets were frequently used in Presentation quilts, where a characteristic basket might indicate such regional styles as the Baltimore Album and Baltimore Friendship quilts. Even children were entranced by baskets and used them to create such charmingly simple quilts as that in 31-2, done by schoolchildren for their teacher. Flowers, of course, were also displayed in containers other than baskets, and the use of urns (31-3) or flower pots (31-5), both substantial receptacles for flowers, gives a certain solidity to floral motifs.

Within each group of containers—baskets, urns, pots, and even cornucopias—one should note the many different kinds that are depicted. Some have handles, others do not; some baskets appear to have an open weave, others are quite tightly woven; some urns are simple in design, others are more ornamental in form; some containers are very realistically rendered, while others are quite primitive. But each of them not only blends in with the design for which it was created, but anchors the overall pattern in place as well.

31-O Baskets of Flowers (color plate)
Virginia, c. 1880
Cotton, 90" x 87"

The basket shape seen in this quilt is the basic form used whether in appliquéd or pieced work. The tulips in the baskets and those interspersed around the edge enliven the design. **(B)**

Judith and James Milne
New York, NY

31-1 Flower Baskets
Baltimore, Maryland, date unknown
Silk and cotton, 94" x 87"
Made by Mrs. Mary Jane Green Maran

Baskets that appear to be woven are filled with fruit and flowers in a very artistic manner. Each basket is enclosed by a stuffed strawberry vine, and the entire design is framed in a soft-green leaf border with a fringe. **(D)**

Smithsonian Institution
Washington, DC

31-1

31-2 Flower Pots
New York, c. 1930
Cotton, 50" x 36"

31-2

This crib quilt, created as a school project and done by children whose names are signed in many of the squares, features baskets done in crayon with appliquéd flowers in the primary colors. The entire design is separated by a green print grid. **(C)**

Just Us
Tucson, AZ

31-3

31-3 Floral Urn
Iowa, c. 1856
Cotton, 82" sq.

A profusion of flowers and fruits in shades of raspberry, pink, yellow, and green are arranged like an appliquéd painting. A variety of needlework techniques—trapunto, reverse appliqué, piping, embroidery, and stuffed work—are illustrated in this quilt. **(E)**

Private Collection

31-4

31-4 Flowers in Baskets
York County, Pennsylvania, dated 1861
Cotton, 84" x 81"
Made by Jenne Cleland

Fanciful flowers in stylized baskets, a floral border, and small red and yellow birds with green wings fill a white field of beautiful quilting. Four red, orange, and green tulips in the center frame enclose the quilter's name and the date March 21, 1861. (C)

Jonathan and Gail Holstein
New York, NY

31-5 Thistle in Flowerpots
Massachusetts, c. 1870
Cotton, 96" x 90"

Green leaves with yellow flowers, red center with yellow and red buds. Yellow edge on tip of thistle. Green vine border with hand-quilted background with yellow-gold tape. This pattern is sometimes interpreted as a cactus. (C)

Kelter-Malcé Antiques
New York, NY

31-6 Baskets of Flowers
Ohio, c. 1842
Cotton, 84" sq.

Three rows of floral designs fill the center of this quilt. Alternating bouquets are placed in baskets of a green print which is also used for the leaves and stems. On the four sides of the quilt are large baskets in red with flowers and vines spreading out around the edges of the quilt. (C)

31-7 Flower Baskets
Illinois, c. 1880
Cotton, 86" sq.

Four large baskets filled with flowers resembling peonies are placed in the four sections of the quilt and are surrounded by a variety of vines with leaves and buds. The white background of the quilt is done in diagonal line quilting. (B)

31-8 Peony in Flower Pot
Mississippi, c. 1850
Cotton, 84" sq.

Brightly-colored peonies and buds on stems of green are placed in flowerpots of green and are surrounded by a swag and bow border. (B)

32 | Wreaths

From the laurel wreath worn by Caesar to the floral wreaths placed on the graves of unknown soldiers, the wreath has been symbolic of respect and honor and is frequently used in heraldry. The American needlewoman would have found the wreath a congenial and common element of her design vocabulary, finding it in contemporary furniture design and using it freely and frequently in mourning pictures and other fancywork that drew inspiration from neoclassicism.

For quilters this motif provides a simple and handsome design element whose treatment changes with each needleworker. Some rose wreaths, for example, are composed of flowers and buds (32-2); others may be only rosettes (32-4); some combine such flowers as the rose and the tulip (32-11); or occasionally the wreath may be only buds and leaves.

The colors found in Wreath designs are the same as those used in other floral motifs, with red, pink, and yellow for the flowers and green for the leaves and stem. Some Wreath patterns may be executed in only one or two colors or may be a combination of all four colors.

The design of Wreath quilts permits large areas of the white background to show, and this space is generally filled with quilting patterns that illustrate the skill of the needlewoman who made her quilt.

32-O Wreaths (color plate)
Pennsylvania, c. 1860
Cotton, 82" sq.

A very popular appliqué design, these colorful wreath patterns were often one of the twelve quilts in a young girl's dowry chest.

Thos. K. Woodard Antiques
New York, NY

32-1 Rose of Sharon and Tulip Wreath
Maryland, c. 1860
Cotton, 94" x 91"

Nine beautiful Rose of Sharon and Tulip wreaths in red, yellow, and green fill the center of the quilt while a meandering vine border frames the entire design. **(C)**

Jo Giese Brown
New York, NY

32-2 President's Wreath
New Jersey, c. 1850
Cotton, 96" x 90"

Cherry-red rosettes rest on a deep moss-green wreath set in each corner with green and yellow buds edged in red. A double-leafed vine and bud border meanders around three sides of this quilt. **(C)**

Tewksbury Antiques
Oldwick, NJ

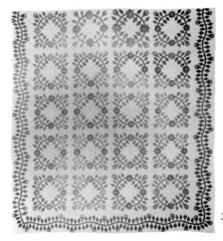

32-2

32-3

32-3 Rose Tree
Place unknown, c. 1840
Cotton, 99″ x 83″
Made by Patience Ramsey

Executed by a 13-year old girl, this design, also known as "Missouri
Rose" and "Prairie Rose," has the half-wreaths on each side in a vertical position to accommodate a narrow bed. Earlier quilts of this pattern would have had the rows of half-wreaths all in a horizontal plane
making a larger square quilt to cover the wider-style beds. The quilt is
pieced and appliquéd on white. **(D)**

Smithsonian Institution
Washington, DC

32-4 Wreath
New York, c. 1885
Cotton, 102" sq.

Red flowers placed on a wreath of green leaves sit in the center of a frame within a frame, surrounded by eight more wreaths also framed with a double border. Quilted to each corner of both frames within this design are repeats of the wreath motif. **(C)**

Mr. and Mrs. Robert J. Bonner
Malone, NY

32-5 Wreath of Roses
Wilkesville, Vinton County, Ohio, c. 1850
Cotton, 82" x 80"
Made by Mary Ann Cutshall Bishop

The quilting is an integral part of the design in this quilt since the cross-hatching on the roses gives them depth, while the double line diagonal quilting through the leaves gives substance to an otherwise flat motif. **(D)**

Smithsonian Institution
Washington, DC

32-6

32-6 Rosette Wreath
Ohio, c. 1870
Cotton, 74" x 90"

Small eyelet-shaped leaves are set in the center of a beige whorl wreath intercepted by a red blade design. Two sides of the border are edged in chevrons. **(C)**

Judith and James Milne
New York, NY

32-7 Rose Wreath
Kentucky, c. 1860
Cotton, 86" x 72"

Similar to many wreath patterns in this design, the small rosettes of red with yellow centers are placed on a circular vine with buds and leaves emanating from it. **(B)**

32-8 Wreath of Roses
New York, c. 1880
Cotton, 84" x 72"

A cluster of small roses in red and pink form a wreath out of which leaves and rose buds protrude. Three rows, each consisting of three rose wreaths, are symmetrically arranged across the face of the quilt which has a scalloped edge and beautiful quilting in the white spaces. **(C)**

32-9 Wreath of Roses
Missouri, c. 1860
Cotton, 86" sq.

A wreath design composed of roses, buds, and leaves is encased in a double-bar grid with a zigzag motif within it. The wreath and grid rest against a white field with beautiful feather quilting in the border. **(C)**

32-10 President's Wreath
Wisconsin, c. 1890
Cotton, 72" sq.

Interlocking circles of rose and leaf wreath pattern in red and green are set against a white background with diagonal-line quilting. This is a rather crowded design that completely fills the center section of the quilt. For a similar quilt see 32-2. **(B)**

32-11

32-11 Dahlia Wreath
New Jersey, c. 1880
Cotton, 84" sq.

In floral designs it is often difficult to distinguish between the various flower motifs, for the rosettes in this pattern closely resemble any number of Rose of Sharon designs. Nine wreath arrangements are neatly placed across the center of the quilt and one framed in a serpentine border composed of elements of the dahlia wreath design. **(C)**

Private Collection

32-12 Wreath of Garden Flowers
Indiana, c. 1859
Cotton, 86" sq.

A sprightly arrangement of garden flowers is entwined to create four wreaths framed with a vine border that is filled with sprigs of flowers and leaves. **(B)**

33 | Leaves

The more one studies quilts, the more intrigued one becomes by what is **not** represented. For example, seldom is a tree illustrated in appliqué work, yet there are a great number of different Leaf designs depicted, often quite realistically interpreted. Some Presentation quilts contain small trees, but one does not generally find them as the main motif of an appliquéd quilt.

A quilt may contain a repeated pattern of one type of leaf appearing almost as if the quilt had been left under a tree on a windy autumn day and the leaves allowed to arrange themselves in an all-over design. In some quilts the leaves are very realistic and resemble oak, maple, elm, poplar, aspen, and the leaves of various fruit trees (33-4). Or they may be quite abstract, stylized, or geometric (33-8).

33-O Leaves (color plate)
Chandlerville, Illinois, c. 1860
Cotton, 88" x 86"
Made by Ernestine Eberhardt Zaumzeil

This botanical garden employs a unique appliqué technique. The same fabric has been used in the vine on the left side as on the right, but reversed to give a lighter shade. The same technique appears in the shades of maple leaves in the center and right-hand corner. The roses are layers of petals built up to give depth. A wonderfully imaginative sense of perspective is achieved by placing tiny animals juxtaposed to large leaves in the center. **(D)**

George E. Schoellkopf Gallery
New York, NY

33-1 Leaves
Pennsylvania, c. 1860
Cotton, 37" x 36"

In this cradle quilt, olive-green buds and leaves surround a red polka-dotted center. This same red fabric is used in the tassel and bow border which is separated with olive-green swags. **(C)**

Phyllis Haders
New York, NY

33-2 Leaves with Poinsettias
Virginia, c. 1860
Cotton, 79" x 78"

Red poinsettias interspersed with blue leaves are unified by stems of red and blue berries against a white field edged in a light-green tape. **(B)**

Kelter-Malcé Antiques
New York, NY

33-3 Oak Leaf
Place unknown, c. 1860
Cotton, 77½" x 73½"
Made by Sarah Ann Mullon

Employing a simple motif of leaves and berries, this quilt displays a lovely balanced design, with the main motif picked up in a meandering vine border. **(C)**

Smithsonian Institution
Washington, DC

33-4 Leaves
Ohio, c. 1870
Cotton, 68" x 66"

Large leaf designs in green and red make a botanical sampler placed on a white background. Written on the quilt are the names of

33-4

three towns: Hope and Newton, New Jersey, and Canton, Connecticut. The name "Ellen" has been chain stitched in the center. **(C)**

Jay Johnson
New York, NY

33-5

33-5 Leaves
Virginia, dated 1855
Cotton, 86″ x 85″

Abstract leaves in calicoes and plaids of reds, pinks, blues, yellows, and grey are arranged in sixteen squares separated by four curry-colored squares with the same color used for the double frame border. **(C)**

Judith and James Milne
New York, NY

33-6 Leaf Variation
Massachusetts, c. 1890
Cotton, 88" sq.

This colorful top, or summer spread, has a sampling of appliqué motifs. Squared off by a red grid are heart-shaped leaves with a border of blue leaves hung with red and yellow baskets. The center square with the sprightly red horse has small red and yellow rosettes sprinkled against a white background, and the basket motif appears again on each side of the border. **(C)**

Kelter-Malcé Antiques
New York, NY

33-7 Leaves
New York, c. 1880
Cotton, 78" sq.

Stylized leaves of red and white are set against contrasting squares. Simple quilting reinforces the design. **(A)**

Judith and James Milne
New York, NY

33-8 Ferns and Leaves
Pennsylvania, c. 1870
Cotton, 98" x 80"

Fern leaves of orange and olive green interspersed with abstract leaves of yellow and bright pink are applied to a printed background. **(A)**

Judith and James Milne
New York, NY

33-9 Hickory Leaf
Marcellus, New York, c. 1858
Cotton, 88" x 85"
Made by Annis Lawrence Curtis

Blue cotton print on white background with diagonal quilting composes the pattern also popularly known as "Reel" or "Orange Peel." **(B)**

Smithsonian Institution
Washington, DC

33-10 Peapod Leaf
Probably Pennsylvania, c. 1880
Cotton, 79" x 86"

Moss-green appliquéd leaves are enclosed in a chocolate-brown sawtooth design on white diamonds against a soft pink background. Three sides of the border are in a green print with a pencil-point-thin red calico edging. **(B)**

Phyllis Haders
New York, NY

33-11 Tea Leaves
Virginia, c. 1850
Cotton, 72" sq.

A multitude (256) of leaf motifs that resemble the lily-like flower in 30-18 cover the surface. The leaves are green against a white background, making a strikingly handsome design. **(C)**

33-12 Oak Leaf
Missouri, c. 1880
Cotton, 86" x 72"

A dark-blue print is used for the oak leaves that are arranged in a pattern similar to 33-9. The border is a very simple leaf design in the form of a teardrop on a white field. **(B)**

33-13 Oak Leaf and Currant
Indiana, c. 1860
Cotton, 86" x 84"

A pattern of four oak leaves form a cross whose stems join to create a diamond that is encircled by a ring of currants. The brown leaves, red currants, and a green vine and leaf border make this a colorful quilt. **(B)**

34 | Feathers

In some instances the Feather pattern so closely resembles the Leaf design that the two are placed side by side in this book for ready reference and comparison. The simplest Feather design consists of four-feathered prongs radiating straight out from the center (color plate 34). More complex designs (34-2) double the number of feathers and curve them gracefully, almost suggesting a whirling feathered pinwheel.

The use of the Feather design is an easy way to fill the large area of a quilt with color. Two of the more frequently used color combinations in this pattern are blue feathers on a mustard background and red feathers on white. In addition to its use as a popular appliqué pattern, the Feather motif is frequently used as a quilting stitch (45-1).

34-0 Feathers (Princess Feather) (color plate)
Michigan, c. 1880
Cotton, 78" sq.

The pumpkin-colored background makes an interesting contrast to the red and blue feather and circle designs in this quilt. **(C)**

Sandra Mitchell
Southfield, MI

34-1 Feather Variation
Pennsylvania, c. 1870
Cotton, 84" sq.

An individual touch is lent to this typical pattern by the lyres resting in

34-1

leaf motifs along the border. The "feathers" in the four clusters closely resemble leaves in their design. **(C)**

Sandra Mitchell
Southfield, MI

34-2

34-2 Princess Feather
Pennsylvania, c. 1880
Cotton, 108" sq.

Alternating red and tan feathers are pinned to the white background by a red and tan flower center. Red vines terminating in tan buds wend their way among the feathers and swags. A minute sawtooth design hugs the border. **(C)**

Cherishables
Washington, DC

34-3 Princess Feather
Illinois, c. 1880
Cotton, 69" sq.

Turkey-red feathers with a white spine held in place by a small white circle are set on a white field with simple quilting. A red picket border frames the quilt. **(B)**

Judith and James Milne
New York, NY

34-4 Princess Feather
Pennsylvania, c. 1880
Cotton, 88" sq.

A center medallion motif of eight-pronged feather designs in red is surrounded by flowerpots containing flower buds and Princess Feather leaves. **(B)**

34-5 Princess Feather
Michigan, c. 1880
Cotton, 72" x 69"

Brown feather motifs radiate from a red six-pointed star. There are four of these designs on a white background, with individual feathers forming a border around the design. **(B)**

34-6 Princess Feather
Ohio, c. 1840
Cotton, 84" sq.

Four green feathers form a pinwheel design interspersed with green, red, and yellow tulips. A meandering vine border frames the design. **(B)**

34-7 Princess Feather
Ohio, c. 1850
Cotton, 86" x 74"

A very quiet Princess Feather design in red and green is given movement by a meandering leaf border out of which maple leaves protrude. **(B)**

34-8 Princess Feather
Indiana, c. 1835
Cotton, 86" sq.

From a star center, the feather motif radiates in pinwheel fashion against a white background. The colors of this design are a soft dull green and rose, more subtle colors than one usually finds in this pattern. **(B)**

34-9 Feather and Rose
Kentucky, c. 1880
Cotton, 82" x 78"

A red rose center is surrounded by green feathers in a pinwheel design placed in three rows across the quilt. A scalloped border with small rosettes at each of the indentations of the swag make a lively frame for this busy design. **(B)**

35 | Buildings

Of all the buildings of the 19th century and the early years of the 20th, the one that conjures up the most nostalgic image is the "Little Red Schoolhouse" filled with girls in calico dresses and mischievous barefoot boys wrestling with the demands of the "three R's" in their **McGuffey's Eclectic Readers.** Certainly the number of quilts in the "Schoolhouse" pattern attests to the importance that school days played in the lives of these quilters. The design is almost always basically the same—a side view of the building, with or without a bell tower or cupola (35-2).

As one might expect, other buildings frequently depicted on quilts include the church and the barn. Occasionally, an entire village is shown (color plate 35). Appliquéd buildings could be done in solid-colored fabrics or in a multitude of different printed materials, which might be pieced as in 35-2.

35-0 Buildings (Houses and Barns) (color plate)
Massachusetts, c. 1910
Cotton, 88" x 84"

Effective use is made of calicoes and ginghams to simulate the brick, stone, and wood construction of these buildings. Several of the barns and houses are pictured in mirror image. **(C)**

Anne Weld Crawford
New York, NY

35-1 Schoolhouse
Cincinnati, Ohio, dated 1890
Cotton, 78" x 72"

Each schoolhouse is done in a different fabric, but employing the same design. In the white space between the roof and wall are the signatures of the quilters. Around several of the chimneys are embroidered horseshoes, and various dates in 1890. A blue and white calico grid separates the schoolhouses. **(C)**

Sandra Mitchell
Southfield, MI

35-2 Houses
Ohio, c. 1870
Cotton, 80" x 72"

Geometrically-conceived houses in printed fabrics are surrounded by a sawtooth edge and calico border. **(C)**

Phyllis Haders
New York, NY

35-3 Schoolhouses
Probably New York, c. 1925
Cotton and satin, 75" sq.

Light-blue houses with pink doors and windows support deep-red

35-3

roofs. Red bars frame each house and a deep-blue border frames the design. **(B)**

Darwin D. Bearley
Akron, OH

35-4

35-4 Schoolhouse
Ohio, c. 1920
Cotton, 78" x 69"

These light-grey houses with two bright-red chimneys sit in white squares with feather-wreath quilting over each house. A bright sea-blue border and grid are punctuated by Nine-Patch squares. **(B)**

Esprit De Corp
San Francisco, CA

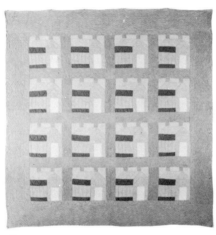

35-5

35-5 Schoolhouse
Pennsylvania, c. 1900
Cotton, 81" sq.

These khaki-green houses, with beige roofs quilted to resemble shingles, have double coral chimneys and light-pink front doors. Thin coral strips hold a blue grid. Lined twisted quilting is on the outer blue border. **(B)**

Sandra Mitchell
Southfield, MI

35-6 Schoolhouse
Place unknown, c. 1890
Cotton, 80" sq.

Brightly-colored fabrics form a variety of barns which closely resemble Log Cabins in construction. They are set in a wide blue grid. **(B)**

35-7 Schoolhouse
New Hampshire, c. 1880
Cotton, 77" x 76"

A grid of chintz separates the schoolhouses that are framed in white, giving the impression of a picture album. An interesting aspect of this quilt is that the four center views of the schoolhouse are of its side, while the twelve squares surrounding them depict the front of the school-house. **(B)**

36 | Figures

"Sunbonnet Sue" (color plate 36), her companion "Overall Bill" (36-1) or "Sam" as he was also known, and the "Colonial Lady" began to be popular patterns in the first quarter of the 20th century. These little figures appear in rows across the quilt and are sometimes framed in a grid. Their faces are usually covered by a hat, and variation occurs with the use of accessories—parasols and purses for the girls and hoes and other farm implements for the boys. Dressed in plaids, calicoes, ginghams, and solid-colored fabrics, these figures cannot help but evoke a smile from the viewer as they "parade" across the face of the quilts hidden behind their big hats.

Appliqué animals began to appear on quilts at about this time, too, and were particularly charming on crib quilts. Such a playful quilt is described in 36-6, but is not illustrated.

36-0 Figures (Sunbonnet Sue) (color plate)
Pennsylvania, c. 1920
Cotton, 76" x 74"

There is always something charming and appealing about these faceless ladies under their floppy hats as they parade to market, several of them prepared for inclement weather, while the others swing their purses. **(B)**

Private Collection

36-1 Overall Bill
Ohio, c. 1920
Cotton, 86" x 76"

These nonchalant companions to Sunbonnet Sue (color plate 36) wear solid-colored overalls with calico shirts and matching hats in pastel shades and red. Each of these boys is separated by a light-blue grid ending in a scalloped border. **(A)**

My Friend and Me
Akron, OH

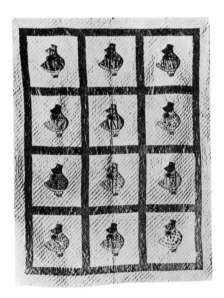

36-2 Sunbonnet Baby
Illinois, c. 1900
Cotton, 86″ x 80″

These Sunbonnet Babies in their ruffled petticoats, calico dresses, and sunbonnets seem to be turned with their backs to a breeze as their dresses are raised just enough to glimpse the petticoats. **(A)**

Private Collection

36-3 Sunbonnet Lassies
Missouri, c. 1910
Cotton, 74" x 68"

These young ladies are having an earnest conversation by the garden gate while birds fly overhead and large sunflowers "grow" in the garden. An interesting border frames the design. **(B)**

Private Collection

36-4 Sunbonnet Ladies
Illinois, c. 1910
Cotton, 42" x 36"

A pair of Sunbonnet Ladies chat on the top and bottom of this crib quilt while three ladies on each side of the quilt pass the time of day. They are dressed in dark cotton prints, and one lady in each group carries a parasol. Four pink frames enclose the design placed on a white background with diagonal-line quilting. **(B)**

36-5 Pajama Children
Missouri, c. 1910
Cotton, 42" x 36"

A crib quilt, with a design of pajama-clad children pointing to stars in the center of the quilt, is framed with a border of trees in large tubs resting against a scalloped edge. **(B)**

36-6 Animal Crackers
Missouri, c. 1930
Cotton, 42" x 36"

A grid pattern of blue separates squares filled with a whole array of animals; bears, camels, squirrels, lions, horses, elephants, dogs, and buffalos are enbroidered on a white background. **(A)**

37 | Birds

Just as the pieced quilt seems to demand birds that are geometrically conceived (see section 11), the appliquéd quilt almost always renders birds realistically.

Of all the birds that appear in appliqué—as well as in all 19th-century American arts and crafts—none appears with more frequency than the eagle. Symbolic of freedom and power, the eagle has been a patriotic American emblem since it was incorporated as part of the Great Seal of the United States by Congress in 1782. The eagle, consequently, appears in statuary, powder flasks, drums, door knockers, glassware, china, coverlets, and quilts. Soaring (color plate 37) or at rest (37-1), this majestic bird was used as a design motif on quilts in all periods, but especially during times of political strife—the War of 1812, the War with Mexico, and the Civil War.

Birds frequently appear in Presentation quilts; most popular is, of course, the eagle, but other species are also illustrated. Lest one think that the figure of a bird is always central to the quilt employing such motifs, 32-4 presents twenty-one birds in silhouette that provide a frame for the otherwise non-avian central design.

37-O Birds (Eagles) (color plate)
Cherry Tree, Pennsylvania, c. 1875
Cotton, 78" x 76"

Nine large eagles are followed in flight by twenty-four smaller ones that lack only talons to be identical to those in the center. Beautiful running feather quilting is visible between the rows of birds. **(C)**

Sandra Mitchell
Southfield, MI

37-1 Nine Eagles
Western Ohio, c. 1855
Cotton, 81" sq.

Eagles with olive-green bodies and wings, red heads, and red and yellow tails are framed by an olive-green and red border. Light-green banners wave above the eagles' heads. **(C)**

Darwin D. Bearley
Akron, OH

**37-2 Eagles
Centre County, Pennsylvania,
c. 1850
Cotton, 85" sq.**

Eagles with grey tails and heads, gold bodies, and red wings form a square around a floral wreath. Small red rosettes are scattered about the design. **(C)**

Darwin D. Bearley
Akron, OH

**37-3 Eagle Quilt
Pennsylvania, c. 1900
Cotton, 78" sq.**

Four eagles with red heads and tails, orange-red bodies, and grey wings hover around a red, grey, and orange serrated wheel on a white field. The design is boxed in by a red and orange sawtooth on grey. **(C)**

Phyllis Haders
New York, NY

**37-4 Twenty-One Birds
Probably Ohio, c. 1880
Cotton, 88" x 78"**

Red and blue birds encircling a blue floral design punctuated with red maple leaves on top and bottom. A cluster of three red stars in each corner—all set on a white background in diamond quilting. **(C)**

Private Collection

37-5 Birds in Flight
Michigan, c. 1920
Cotton, 85" x 72"

An oriental mood is communicated by a stylized white bird migrating across a light blue sky under a pink blooming cherry tree, a pattern repeating and alternating with a second motif. Fans with accents of blue and white sprigs unify this design. **(B)**

Judith and James Milne
New York, NY

38 | Fruit

In referring to the strawberry, someone once remarked: "Doubtless God could have made a better berry, but doubtless God never did." Perhaps this idea of the strawberry as the perfect fruit occurred to the quilters of the two strawberry quilts (38-1 and 38-2) in this section, both of which are completely different in their interpretations of this delicious fruit. The one is abstract, with every detail beautifully stylized. This closeness of detail might have been done in anticipation of augmenting the design with stuffed work, as shown in detail in

43-4. By contrast, the second quilt has very artistically-arranged, lush red strawberries that appear to have been just plucked from the vine.

A favorite fruit for appliquéd quilts is the grape (38-3) which is frequently stuffed to more nearly resemble the actual fruit. The grape and/or its leaves often appear as a meandering vine border on many quilts.

A playful design depicting fruit is illustrated in color plate 38, where some baskets are overflowing with apples, pineapples, and grapes while other pieces of fruit "float" across the face of the quilt.

38-O Fruit (Baskets of Fruit) (color plate)
Indiana, c. 1870
Cotton, 75" x 66"

The luscious fruit spilling out of the basket and floating in the design is appliquéd to a white field enclosed by a light beige grapevine. **(C)**

Mr. and Mrs. Henry Rutkowski
Detroit, MI

38-1

38-1 Strawberry
Missouri, c. 1835
Cotton, 92" x 90"

Clusters of large strawberry plants, whose fruit is alternating rows of pink and red, rest in minute green pots with small red and orange bands on them. Beautifully executed trapunto strawberries fill the four white spaces in the main section of the design. Cross-hatched quilting creates a pronounced border. **(C)**

Phyllis Haders
New York, NY

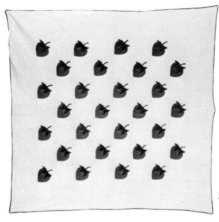

38-2

38-2 Strawberries
Medina, Ohio, c. 1900
Cotton, 85″ x 75″

Luscious red strawberries are arranged in a very geometrical pattern against a white field. **(B)**

Darwin D. Bearley
Akron, OH

38-3

38-3 Martha's Vineyard
Knox County, Tennesse, c. 1880
Cotton, 89″ x 72″

Clusters of grapes, artfully balanced off center, are joined by extended vines and encircled by a meandering grapevine border. Quilting in the white spaces repeats the appliquéd motif. **(B)**

Goose Tracks Antiques
Knoxville, TN

38-4 Strawberries
Tennessee, c. 1880
Cotton, 84" sq.

Strawberries growing out of very straight stalks appear more like flowers than a strawberry vine. The red and orange fruit is very angular in design, giving a decided geometric cast to this methodically-arranged fruit pattern. **(B)**

38-5 Grapevine
Louisiana, c. 1855
Cotton, 86" sq.

Two and sometimes three grapevines of a dull brown, filled with stuffed purple printed-fabric grapes and leaves of a green print, create a rich and luscious deep border on three sides of the quilt. The center is arranged with delicate sprigs of a variety of floral motifs. **(C)**

38-8 Love Apple
Ohio, c. 1850
Cotton, 88" x 72"

Two vertical rows of love apples (tomatoes) of deep red with a lighter red center and green leaves are framed with a serpentine ribbon border with a fleur-de-lis motif "growing" out of it. Beautiful whorl quilting alternates with the rows of love apples. **(C)**

39 Hawaiian Quilts

Although the so-called "Hawaiian" quilt was frequently made on the tropical islands that give the quilt its name, the technique used in making it was sometimes employed in other locales on the American mainland, especially in the areas settled by the Pennsylvania Germans.

Hawaiian quilt patterns are made by folding pieces of paper in fourths, cutting the design to resemble a snowflake or other form, and transferring this design onto a white piece of fabric. The technique is called "scherenschnitte," a Pennsylvania-German term meaning "scissor cut" or silhouetted, that aptly describes the manner in which these beautiful lacy designs are created. These large appliqué patterns, most often done in color, are a stunning contrast to the plain background.

Called kapa lau by the Hawaiians, these quilts were considered by their Hawaiian makers appropriate only for use on beds. Motifs are inspired by foliage, fruit, and flowers of the Pacific Islands.

39-O Hawaiian (color plate)
Hawaii, c. 1860
Cotton, 78" x 61"

An abstract red floral design is framed on top and bottom by a vine capped at each end by a fleur-de-lis. Fan quilting gives texture to the red cloth. **(C)**

Phyllis Haders
New York, NY

39-1 Hawaiian-type
Ephrata, Pennsylvania, c. 1880
Cotton, 86" x 85"

A soft azalea pink set against a hunter green creates an unusual color combination for this typical Hawaiian pattern. **(C)**

Jonathan and Gail Holstein
New York, NY

39-2 Hawaiian
Hawaii, c. 1900
Cotton, 85" sq.

Plant motifs of stylized pineapples appear throughout this typically Hawaiian pattern done in olive green against a white background. **(C)**

Stella Rubin
Darnestown, MD

39-2

40 | Crazy Quilts

The Crazy quilt is said by some to have been the very earliest kind of quilt, as its random patterns, utilizing any leftover fabrics, can be quickly assembled. Be this as it may, the Crazy quilt should by no means be considered a lowly entity in the world of quilts. On the contrary, these quilts are very much part of the Victorian era, an age of opulence when they were used not only as bed coverings, but frequently as throws for sofas.

Almost anything was "fodder" for Crazy quilts—silks, satins, velvets, lace, embroidery, painted pictures; designs of people, animals, flowers, and leaves. Some of these quilts are organized into squares (40-2) and are even referred to as "Tile Quilts" (40-5), indicating of course the presence of a grid. Others, as their name implies, are just plain crazy, with no apparent overall design. Yet even the most chaotic-appearing quilt must have been well thought-out for all of these motifs to have been incorporated into a single work.

Perhaps more than any other kind of quilt, Crazy quilts tell a "story," and it is fun to look at them and imagine what all the designs might possibly represent.

40-0 Crazy (color plate)
New York, dated 1888
Silk and velvet, 50" sq.

A grid organizes these fractured bits of fabric into squares. Fans in each corner and in the central square give a theme to the quilt. The date appears in the second square from the right in the second row. **(B)**

Phyllis Haders
New York, NY

40-1 Crazy Blocks
Place unknown, c. 1880
Velvet and silks, 64½" x 61⅜"

This is a slumber throw of Baby Blocks pattern in the center with a crazy patched border squared with floral arrangements in each corner. The design is held in place with a variety of embroidery stitches. **(C)**

Smithsonian Institution
Washington, DC

40-2 Crazy
Baltimore, Maryland, c. 1890
Silk, 73" sq.
Made by Augusta Elizabeth Duvall

This slumber throw, composed of nine large squares, was made by a botanist who decorated her quilt with a great variety of embroidered plants. **(C)**

Smithsonian Institution
Washington, DC

40-2

40-3

40-3 Crazy
Place unknown, c. 1880
Silk, 73" sq.

This elaborately embroidered slumber throw is initialed "JK." Holding this Crazy design in place is a colorful striped border. **(C)**

Smithsonian Institution
Washington, DC

40-4 Crazy
Pennsylvania, c. 1890
Wool, 76" sq.

40-4

Alternating stripes of gold and midnight-blue create a geometric border for this squared-off crazy quilt pattern of bright shades of reds and blues. **(B)**

Sandra Mitchell
Southfield, MI

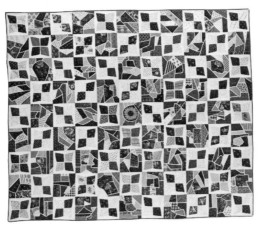

40-5

40-5 Crazy (Tile)
Pennsylvania, c. 1880
Cotton, 86″ x 80″

Colorful odd-shaped fabrics are placed in squares to resemble tiles.

Beautiful chintzes and calicoes are found in this quilt. (See details in 40-6.) **(B)**

Sandra Mitchell
Southfield, MI

40-6

40-6 Crazy (Tile) (detail)

Irregular shaped fabrics depicting blush-pink rose against a black background, a white bird etched onto a brilliant red background, and a blue and yellow paisley print with other colorful calicoes and chintzes are combined to create this single tile design.

Sandra Mitchell
Southfield, MI

40-7 Crazy
Massachusetts, c. 1890
Satin and velvet, 64" x 63"

A recurring fan motif gives a unifying theme to this quilt whose center square is made of fabric from Abigail Adams's wedding dress. The lower left square has a midnight-blue background with bright flowers and a yellow bird which is balanced by the bright Chinese-red background color of the upper-right square. **(B)**

Detroit Historical Museum
Detroit, MI

40-7

40-8

40-8 Crazy
Vermont, c. 1885
Silk and velvet, 72″ sq.

A collection of needlework techniques is evident in this quilt; pieced work, appliqué, embroidery, monogramming. Unfortunately lost to posterity is the significance of each of these squares. **(B)**

Private Collection

40-9 Crazy
Indiana, c. 1890
Flannel, 80" x 71"

Squares composed of odd-shapes of red, blue, maroon, black, and green fabric are joined by turkey or fly stitch embroidery. **(A)**

Private Collection

40-10 Stained Glass Crazy
Pennsylvania, c. 1925
Wool, 81" sq.

Raspberry border squared off with indigo holds "stained glass" squares on a soft pink background. Edged in indigo, squares are of primary and brown colors. Whorl quilting makes up the background. **(A)**

Esprit De Corp
San Francisco, CA

41 | Presentation Quilts

Included in this category are Friendship, Album, Autograph, Bride's, as well as Presentation quilts. Although known by many names, these were usually quilts made by friends and then presented as a gift to some fortunate recipient. Some of these quilts—the Bride's quilt or a Presentation quilt given to a minister and his wife upon their departure from their parish—were made for special occasions.

During the Civil War, flag quilts with the names of friends inscribed in stars were given to young women whose beaux entered military service. Presentation quilts are usually filled with symbols—religious, patriotic, and fraternal, the meanings of which are sometimes lost to us today. Even the rebus—a word or phrase spelled out in pictures, and a particularly popular Victorian parlor pastime—is to be found in some Presentation quilts (41-6).

41-0 Presentation (color plate)
Maryland, c. 1845
Cotton, 89" sq.

The painterly quality of appliqué is particularly evident in the delicate design of this quilt. The gradations of color in the eagle, and small blue flowers in the bouquet at the end of the row in which it sits, seem more to be done with the brush than the needle. The floral bouquet in the upper-left corner has a freshness of design in contrast to the square next to it that appears almost mystical in interpretation. **(E)**

Sandra Mitchell
Southfield, MI

41-1 Friendship
New York, c. 1875
Cotton, 84" sq.

This summer spread features a potpourri of textiles cut into birds, flowers, leaves, and baskets embellished with silk embroidery. **(C)**

Just Us
Tucson, AZ

41-1

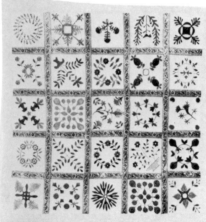

41-2

41-2 Friendship
Maryland, c. 1845
Cotton, 96" sq.

Strips of red and yellow chintz form a grid emcompassing a variety of typical floral and leaf appliqué motifs set against a white field with small cube quilting. **(C)**

Private Collection

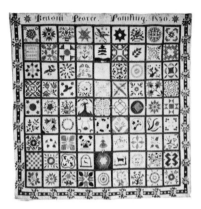

41-3 Friendship
Pawling, New York, dated 1850
Cotton, 103" sq.
Made by Friends of Benoni Pearce

This large quilt of eighty-one squares has many typical designs of both pieced and appliquéd work. A floral border on three sides is offset by the fourth side, giving the name of the recipient, place, and date in Gothic lettering. **(D)**

Smithsonian Institution
Washington, DC

41-4 Friendship
Kentucky, c. 1930
Cotton, 80" x 64"

A triple grid of green, pink, and purple is anchored at the crossbars by a Nine-Patch design. Many of the squares are filled with appliquéd ladies, birds, baskets or flowers and the other squares are in popular pieced designs—Jacob's Ladder, Monkey Wrench, Flocks of Birds, and a Four Patch. **(C)**

Linda Leddick
Detroit, MI

41-4

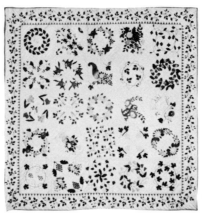

41-5

41-5 Bride's Quilt
Caroll County, Maryland, c. 1850-51
Cotton, 92" sq.
Made by Elizabeth Jane Baile

This quilt of flowers and fruit motifs, some of which are outlined in
button-hole stitch, with predominant colors of red and green on white

with a sawtooth and padded strawberry border, was made by Elizabeth Jane Baile who married Levi Monahan on October 30, 1851: Embroidered on quilt: "Commenced June, 1850, Finished Oct. 30, 1851." **(D)**

Smithsonian Institution
Washington, DC

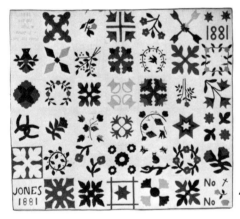

41-6

41-6 Presentation
New York, dated 1881
Cotton, 81" x 70"

A wonderful array of typical appliqué motifs cover this quilt made for the Rev. J.F. Jones and his wife. **(D)**

Collection of Jones New York at Home
New York, NY

41-7 Presentation
Maltaville, New York, c. 1847
Cotton, 93" x 91"
Made by Ladies of the Presbyterian Church

Each square is signed by its maker. The center square contains a poem about friendship encircled with a wreath of flowers. Beautiful quilting covers the white spaces around the leaves, flowers, and bird designs. **(E)**

Smithsonian Institution
Washington, DC

41-7

41-8

41-8 Presentation
Elizabeth Port, New Jersey, dated 1852
Cotton, 101" x 100"
Made by the Women and Children of the Methodist Episcopal
**   Church**

This beautiful quilt contains a great variety of popular appliqué motifs, many of which would have had significance to the missionaries to whom it was given. The hands with the heart and hammer are symbols of the Odd Fellows fraternal organization. The church at the center of the third row is a replica of the one in Elizabeth Port. The Bible, Noah's arc and the wise man on the camel carry obvious religious connotations. **(E)**

Museum of American Folk Art
New York, NY

41-9

41-9 Album
Place unknown, c. 1860
Cotton, 89¾" x 85¼"

Twenty-five blocks make up this quilt which includes floral designs, flower baskets and vases, a valentine heart with bow and arrows, and symbols of faith hope and charity (cross, heart, and anchor). Two patriotic emblems are the eagle in the upper-left corner and the United States shield and stars at the center. A brown and green leaf border frames the design. **(D)**

Shelburne Museum
Shelburne, VT

41-10 Album Sampler
Ohio, c. 1914
Cotton, 82" x 74"

A lively assortment of floral and geometric motifs of reds, golds, and light green are bound by a burgundy and gold border with a red edge. In the quilting are birds, flowers, hearts, scissors, hands, and the signatures of a variety of quilters. **(D)**

Judith and James Milne
New York, NY

41-10

41-11

41-11 Album
Shrewsbury, New Jersey, c. 1845
Cotton, 101" x 97"

Forty-nine squares of earth tones set in a muted orange grid compose this rather large quilt. Most of the squares are signed in the centers. **(B)**

New Jersey State Museum
Trenton, NJ

42 | **Patriotic Quilts**

As the new American nation emerged and developed, patriotic events were frequently recorded by quilters. New states admitted to the Union (42-2), presidential campaigns (42-3), and various expositions—including the Centennial (color plate 42), the Columbian, and the Century of Progress—all inspired patriotic designs for appliquéd quilts. Flags, the eagle, and famous political figures were immortalized in Patriotic quilts of red, white, and blue.

Some of these quilts incorporate souvenirs appropriate to a given event—such as handkerchiefs or memorabilia from the Centennial (color plate 42). In order to reinforce the point expressed in a Patriotic quilt, its visual message was frequently embroidered with sayings, mottoes, or quotations.

42-O Patriotic (Centennial) (color plate)
Massachusetts, c. 1876
Cotton, 76½" x 73"
Made by Esther Elizabeth Cooley

The maker of this quilt collected mementos from the Centennial exhibition which she had attended and patterned them into this patriotic design. It shows the seal of the Centennial surrounded by American flags and smaller flags of other countries represented at the exhibit. **(D)**

Smithsonian Institution
Washington, DC

42-1 Patriotic
Kansas, c. 1861
Cotton, 36" sq.

A symmetrically conceived background and border support a lopsided star filled with stars and embroidered with the word "Baby" in the center. **(C)**

Museum of American Folk Art
New York, NY

42-2 Patriotic
Probably Texas, c. 1846
Cotton, 82" sq.

Twenty-eight stars in the center square may indicate that the quilt was made in recognition of the admission to the Union in 1845, of the 28th state, Texas. **(C)**

Phyllis Haders
New York, NY

42-3 James K. Polk
Pennsylvania, c. 1844
Cotton, 70" x 74"

This quilt is made up of textile printed broadsides incorporating Polk's name in the American flag. In the center is a picture of the 11th president with the words "JAMES K. POLK" above the picture and "POLK & DALLAS" under it. The flags are set apart with stripes of pale-pink cotton and rectangles of medium-blue cotton. (George M. Dallas was Polk's vice president.) **(D)**

Shelburne Museum
Shelburne, VT

42-4 Patriotic Hawaiian
Hawaii, c. 1897
Cotton, 79" sq.

An emblem of Hawaii is the focal point of this quilt whose design has stripes of grey, red, and white uniting four British flags. **(E)**

Shelburne Museum
Shelburne, VT

42-5 Patriotic
Maine, c. 1860
Cotton, 81" x 71"

Alternating blue and red stars on a white field surround a shield of the United States. **(B)**

42-6 Centennial
Pennsylvania, c. 1876
Cotton, 82" x 74"

The center of this quilt contains a view of "The Memorial Hall Art Gallery" (also seen in color plate 42) and is surrounded by printed fabrics in patriotic motifs of eagles and stars. **(C)**

III White Work

The term "white work," as used in this guide, refers to bed coverings that are a single or double layer of white fabric embroidered, quilted, or tufted with white thread to create a design. On some quilts the fabric may appear to have been dyed or has, in fact, changed color with age. The material employed may be cotton, linen, or wool; examples illustrated in this section, however, are made of cotton, since bed coverings in this material are generally still available to the collector. Since the beauty of white work is determined by the stitching, this section illustrates quilting designs and the ways in which they can be used.

A white work counterpane may be composed of a variety of motifs—Single, Running, Overall, or Stuffed—hence the names of the categories in this section. In addition to these motifs, another form of white work—the Candlewick spread—is described in the Candlewick section of this book (47).

The knowledgeable collector, interested in both quality and value, will pay particular attention to techniques of quilting and will, before making any purchase, ask a series of mental questions. Are there many quilting motifs, or is the quilt filled only in simple background stitches? Does the quilt include raised or stuffed work, which adds a richness to the design? Each category in this part of the guide illustrates various quilting techniques to be found in quilts and directs the collector's attention to where on the quilt these motifs are most likely to appear.

The fine example of a white-work quilt illustrated in color plate III (p. 45) demonstrates a generous sampling of white-work techniques. Incorporating Stuffed Work and Overall, Running, and Single motifs, the quilt was made of cotton in Baltimore in about 1820, measures 63 inches by 54 inches, and is reproduced with the permission of Jo Giese Brown of New York City. A schematic drawing of the quilt appears on the following page, together with identifications of the quilting techniques that make up its component parts.

1. Stuffed Work
2. Overall Motif
3. Running Motif
4. Single Motif

43 | Stuffed Work

A richness of design is added to a plain white quilt by Stuffed Work, which is used most frequently to give depth to fruit or leaves. Two techniques are used to create a Stuffed-Work design. First, two pieces of fabric are sewn together, and the design is outlined in a running stitch. Then a small hole is pierced in the light backing fabric and cotton is stuffed into the design. For vines and other long running motifs, a cord is used to fill the design instead of cotton, but the general procedure is the same.

43-O Stuffed Work (color plate)
Maryland, c. 1812
Cotton, quilt 94" x 85"

The most frequently-found stuffed motifs in white quilts are fruit and floral designs. This raised effect enhances the design which realistically resembles grapes. **(D)**

Smithsonian Institution
Washington, DC

43-1 Stuffed Work
Ohio, c. 1830
Cotton, 45" sq.

Someone spent many hours making this beautiful stuffed-work quilt for a baby. Grapes, rosettes, leaves, and a corded serpentine vine border fill this crib quilt. **(C)**

Darwin D. Bearley
Akron, OH

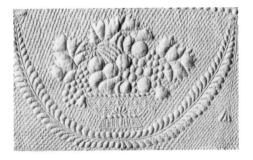

43-2 Stuffed Work (detail)
New York, dated 1861
Cotton, quilt 90" x 88"

A detail from a bride's quilt illustrates the tactile quality of the fruit created by stuffed work.

Private Collection

43-3 Eagle (detail)
Place unknown, c. 1860
Cotton, quilt 95" sq.

This patriotic symbol is greatly enhanced by stuffed work which brings out minute details.

Smithsonian Institution
Washington, DC

43-4 Strawberries (detail)
Missouri, c. 1835
Cotton, quilt 92" x 90"

This stuffed strawberry repeats and greatly enhances the design of the quilt it decorates (see 38-1).

Phyllis Haders
New York, NY

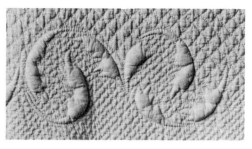

43-5 Stuffed Work (detail)
Brunswick, Maine, c. 1855
Cotton, quilt 89" sq.

Very delicate leaves are raised by the stuffing technique, giving a three-dimensional aspect to the design.

Historic Savannah Foundation
Savannah, GA

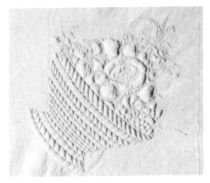

43-6 Fruit Basket (detail)
Place unknown, c. 1860
Cotton, quilt 95" sq.

Luscious stuffed fruit fill a basket that is given depth through the technique of stuffed work.

Smithsonian Institution
Washington, DC

44 | Overall Motif

The Overall Motif, or background quilting, is most important, for it is the stitching that holds the three layers of the quilt in place. Depending on the skill of the quilter, these patterns could be a simple single, double, or triple diagonal line, or a diamond pattern might be used to fasten the quilt more securely.

As a quilter became more and more proficient, she would experiment with elaborate Overall Motifs in the clam shell or fan design. In determining the quality of a quilt, one should look for the small, even stitch that sets apart the skilled quilter from the novice.

44-O Overall Motif (detail) (color plate)
Baltimore, Maryland c. 1820
Cotton, quilt 63" x 54"

Small diamonds, as illustrated in this detail, are a typical background filling or overall motif found in many quilts. This type of filling is more pronounced when done on a solid-color background. (This is a detail from color plate III, p. 36.)

Jo Giese Brown
New York, NY

44-1 Overall Motif (detail)
Brunswick, Maine
Cotton, quilt 89" sq.

One of the most common filling stitches is the square or diaper pattern done in a single-line diagonal stitch.

Historic Savannah Foundation
Savannah, GA

44-2 Overall Motif (detail)
Pennsylvania, dated 1849
Cotton, quilt 93½" x 91½"
Made by Jane Barr

The fine stitching of this mid-century quilt is evident in this detail (taken from 30-24) of an overall pattern.

Smithsonian Institution
Washington, DC

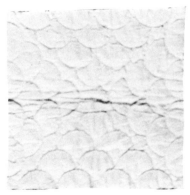

44-3 Overall (Clam Shell) (detail)
New Jersey, c. 1850
Cotton, quilt 96" x 92"

Clam Shell is a popular filling since it can be worked in any direction.
(This is an enlargement of the detail pictured in 12-1.)

Newark Museum
Newark, NJ

45 | Running Motif

Running Motifs are most often found in borders or wending their way
among large floral or geometric designs. The rope and feather designs are the most commonly used. Templates of these patterns
were used to mark out the design on the quilt so that there could be
no mistake in stitching these motifs. Throughout this guide there are
numerous examples of this technique, but perhaps none is more impressive than that seen in the large border of the Amish quilt (see, for
example, 4-1).

45-0 Running Motif (detail) (color)
New Jersey, c. 1820
Cotton, quilt 84" x 78"

This running feather motif makes a handsome filling in borders where it
is most often used.

Kelter-Malcé Antiques
New York, NY

45-1 Running Motif (detail)
Place unknown, c. 1860
Linen, quilt 60" x 35½"

This undulating design is enhanced by a corded vine that separates
and gives depth to a border.

Newark Museum
Newark, NJ

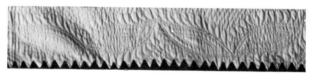

45-2 Running Border (detail)
Ohio, c. 1880
Cotton, quilt 83" x 75½"

In this detail from the pieced quilt "Ocean Waves" (10-11), a feather
edge frames a leaf center. This design zigzags along the border in a
vine-like fashion.

Smithsonian Institution
Washington, DC

45-3 Running (detail)
Ohio, c. 1850
Cotton, quilt 82" x 80"

This running design is a modified elder leaf which works well as a
border around appliquéd or pieced work. (This is a detail of 32-5.)

Smithsonian Institution
Washington, DC

46 | Single Motif

As a magnificent Star fills a pieced quilt, or a huge floral design occupies the center of an appliquéd quilt, a beautifully quilted or stuffed and quilted Single Motif enhances a white-work counterpane. Floral bouquets or baskets of fruit are often the subjects of these designs. In addition to being used as one central focal point, a Single Motif such as the whorl (46-3) will often be repeated throughout the quilt. A Single Motif in the form of a repeated daisy makes an interesting border (46-4).

46-O Single Motif (detail) (color plate)
Baltimore, Maryland, c. 1820
Cotton, quilt 63" x 54"

A single center motif of flowers in a basket is enhanced by stuffed work. Sometimes a single motif is found in the center of a quilt, or it may be repeated in several places in the design. (This is a detail of color plate III, p. 45).

Jo Giese Brown
New York, NY

46-1 Single Motif, (detail)
New York, dated 1861
Cotton, quilt 90" x 88"

Very delicate and sparsely arranged flowers in an urn rest on a doily quilted in the same diaper pattern as the border.

Private Collection

46-2 Single Motif
Pennsylvania, c. 1830
Cotton, 36" x 25"

A very simple and handsome stuffed center medallion design fills this pillow sham. **(C)**

Cherishables
Washington, DC

46-3 Single Motif (detail)
Ohio, c. 1880
Cotton, quilt 83" x 75½"

This whorl motif is frequently used to fill the white spaces left by geometric designs. (This is a detail of 10-10).

Smithsonian Institution
Washington, DC

46-4 Single Motif (detail)
Ohio, dated 1845
Cotton, quilt 86" sq.

A modified daisy framed in a triangle is a single motif which has been repeated across the quilt.

Darwin D. Bearley
Akron, OH

47 | Candlewick Spreads

The Candlewick spread resembles embossed wallpaper in that it has a raised or tufted surface. This surface has an embroidered design made of white wool, cotton, or roving (strands of twisted wool or cotton resembling a candle wick) that pokes through the background material in large raised or looped stitches which are then cut to create a pile or tufting on the spread.

The design of Candlewick spreads usually fills the surface with vines, leaves, fruit, flowers, and swags. Many of these spreads have a fringe border.

47-0 Candlewick (color plate)
Probably Vermont, dated 1819
Homespun, 93" x 83"

The center motif is surrounded by eight small rosettes with four larger ones in each corner encircled by a swag design with four star-like motifs in the corners. More rosettes are placed around the border, united by a meandering vine. Three sides of the spread are edged with fringe. **(D)**

Marston Luce
Washington, DC

47-1 Candlewick
Maine, c. 1820
Cotton, 86" x 76"

Two large central designs, the eagle and flower basket, are simply framed by a very pronounced diamond border. **(D)**

Private Collection

47-2 Candlewick
New Jersey, c. 1890
Cotton, 76″ sq.

A center bouquet is surrounded by a border of grapes and leaves which is, in turn, enclosed by a large meandering vine. A ball and tassel fringe makes a handsome edging on three sides of this spread.
(D)

Private Collection